Britain and the Rise of Communist China

BRITAIN
AND THE RISE OF
COMMUNIST
CHINA

A Study of British Attitudes
1945–1954

BRIAN PORTER

Lecturer in International Politics
University of Wales
Aberystwyth

LONDON
OXFORD UNIVERSITY PRESS
NEW YORK TORONTO
1967

Oxford University Press, Ely House, London W.1.

GLASGOW NEW YORK TORONTO MELBOURNE WELLINGTON
CAPE TOWN SALISBURY IBADAN NAIROBI LUSAKA ADDIS ABABA
BOMBAY CALCUTTA MADRAS KARACHI LAHORE DACCA
KUALA LUMPUR HONG KONG TOKYO

Printed in Great Britain by
The Bowering Press, Plymouth

Contents

Preface

This book is a study of British attitudes, as reflected in Government policy, parliamentary debate, and public opinion, towards the emergence of Communist China as a great power and the issues, wars, and problems which accompanied that momentous event. The period begins with the close of the Second World War, when Chinese Communism revealed itself as a serious contender for the control of China, and ends with the Geneva Conference, when Communist China took rank as a world power and an arbiter in Far Eastern affairs. The first phase of the war in Korea and the last phase of the war in Indo-China have also been included, for even though China herself was but indirectly implicated, these two struggles were so much related to the overall pattern of events that the story would have lost coherence without them.

The Western response to these developments helped to produce the crisis, or succession of crises, which convulsed the Far East and heightened world tension during the greater part of the period. The American side of this response has been well studied; the British side less so. Yet although the British were much less involved in the Far East than were the Americans, British attitudes certainly played a part in determining what happened, and, more vitally, what did not happen.

They helped to determine, also, the state of Anglo-American relations. Greater differences arose between the British and Americans over Far Eastern problems than over any others—apart, perhaps, from the short-lived Suez affair—in which they have been involved since the war. The tensions ran deep and affected opinion at all levels. Indeed the two governments often strained themselves to bridge a gap which grew wider beneath them and which must be understood as much in terms of the differing characters, experiences and traditions of the two nations, as in those of their divergent interests.

Apart, however, from their influence upon international politics, the attitudes described and discussed in these pages have also an intrinsic interest. They tell us much about the

British people half-way through the twentieth century, their
political philosophies, their prejudices and assumptions, their
thoughts about a swiftly changing world and the place of
Britain within that world.

In consequence, division of attitudes according to political
sentiment is a useful approach to a study of this kind, and has
led to the frequent use of the terms 'Tory', 'liberal and radical'
and 'Labour Left' or 'extreme Left'. In writing of the opinion
of the inter-war period, R. B. McCallum was content with two
main categories which he called 'Conservative' and 'Radical'.[1]
With regard to the post-war years, this simple division is no
longer adequate. The tradition of dissent, of basic disagreement
with most of the aims as well as the methods of the orthodox
policy-makers,[2] has, since the war, been mainly confined to the
Leftward quarter or third of the Labour Party. The bulk of the
Party, which itself adopted something of a dissenting position in
the 1930s, has supported an orthodox approach to foreign
policy since 1939.[3] Participation in the wartime coalition, and
the responsibility of power in the years following, helped to
consolidate this change of attitude, so that in the post-war era
the sharpest differences over foreign policy, culminating in the
unilateral disarmament controversy of 1960, and currently revealing themselves in Left-wing condemnation of the Wilson
Government's support for American action in Vietnam, have
occurred within the Labour ranks.

Communist opinion, however, has almost entirely been left
out of account. It was, during these years, a faithful reflection
of the Stalinist line and can therefore tell us nothing of interest
about the British people except that an insignificant number of
them were dedicated supporters of a foreign tyranny. Had the
Russo-Chinese split occurred during this period, British Communist attitudes might have been worth investigating.

Finally, I should like to record my thanks to all who gave me
the benefit of their guidance, criticism or expert knowlege. I
am especially indebted to Professor Martin Wight and Professor Geoffrey Goodwin who supervised the original thesis,
to Mr. G. F. Hudson who examined it and suggested its

[1] *Public Opinion and the Last Peace*, p. x.

[2] See A. J. P. Taylor, *The Trouble Makers: Dissent over Foreign Policy
1792–1939.*   [3] Ibid., pp. 199–200.

publication, and to Mr. A. S. B. Olver who read the work in
typescript and saved me from a number of errors. For particular
information, much of which is embodied in the appendixes, I
have to thank Lord Lindsay of Birker, Mr. Hubert Collar, Miss
Dorothy Woodman, Mr. Arthur Clegg, Lord Chorley, Mr.
Donald Chesworth, Mrs. Joan Mineau and Mr. Kingsley
Martin. I am indebted also to Dr. Durant, Director of Social
Surveys, for permission to reproduce the opinion polls, to Miss
Guéroult, Head Librarian of Whitstable Public Library, for
allowing me to consult some hundredweights of *Hansard* at
home, and to Mrs. Alexander Wheaten, for typing the MS
swiftly and faultlessly while I was abroad. Above all, my grati-
tude must be to my parents, Thomas and Dorothy Porter, who
helped in so many ways and who encouraged and sustained me
throughout.

B. E. P.

Seasalter,
Kent
July 1966

I

The Nature and Rise of Chinese Communism

Towards the end of the Second World War there were few in Britain who had any knowledge of or opinion upon the Chinese Communist movement. Indeed this ignorance extended to China as a whole. The war there had dragged on for so long without any sensational changes of fortune, the distance was so great, the geography so unfamiliar, the political situation so tangled, that not surprisingly less was generally known about the Chinese theatre than about any other. Moreover, apart from a tenuous air-link over the Himalayas, that vast country was effectively cut off from all Western contact. In place of detailed knowledge, a simple stock-view of the Chinese and their leader for the time being prevailed. Such views are commonly held about nations and governments, even amongst the educated, but they flourish especially in time of war. In this instance the Chinese appeared as a tenacious, patient, patriotic peasantry, occupying the honourable place of being the first attacked, and longest resisting, of all the nations allied against militarism and aggression. Their leader, Chiang Kai-shek, was commonly regarded as one of the great men of the age. His success in inspiring his people to continue the struggle, despite immense losses and sufferings, gave him a stature possessed by no other Chinese. He had, moreover, as Sun Yat-sen's successor, a reputation for liberalism, and this, together with his being a convert to Christianity, completed the favourable picture which most British and American people had of him.

In contrast, little was heard of the Chinese Communists. This was a result partly of their inaccessibility in the remote provinces of north China, and partly of the political situation. Civil war between Communists and Nationalists had broken out as early as 1927. When, in 1936, the threat from Japan brought a truce, the Communists agreed to accept Chiang Kai-shek as

nominal leader, but the arrangement was an uneasy one and by
1941 had broken down. In theory the alliance continued, but in
practice the civil war was resumed with sporadic skirmishing.
Since the Communist areas were blockaded by Government
troops, their contact with the outside world was slight.

By early 1945, however, when even the Far Eastern war was
clearly entering its final phase, and when in consequence more
interest was taken in and information supplied about the situation in China, reports began to be received which did not bear
out earlier impressions. The Nationalist régime, it began to be
said, was exhausted and demoralized. Even as late as 1944 the
Japanese, although in retreat on every other front, had managed
to inflict severe defeats upon Chinese Government forces,
capturing much new territory and a number of American airbases recently and laboriously constructed. Although the reputation of Chiang Kai-shek was too great to be seriously affected,
the feeling grew that he stood upon a pyramid of reaction and
corruption.

At the same time a few Western correspondents managed at
last to visit Yenan, the cliff-cave capital of the Communists.
What they saw impressed them. Here was a régime, ultimately
authoritarian perhaps, but in many ways democratic, co-
operating with all classes, distributing land, working efficiently
and honestly, and inspiring enthusiasm. Furthermore, with
little to fight with but home-made or captured weapons, the
Communists had waged a widespread and successful guerrilla
campaign against the Japanese. These findings, not without
some interference from the Chungking censor, were duly com-
municated to the British press, having been worked up in some
cases dispassionately, and in others uncritically and with a
measure of the enthusiasm caught in Yenan.[1]

This is the point we must start from in accounting for the
sympathetic attitude adopted by many in Britain towards
Chinese Communism in the period of its rise. In common with
other left-wing movements Yenan had emerged from the war
with credit. This was so largely because the Second World War

[1] For an authoritative account and perceptive appraisal of the Nationalist
and Communist régimes during 1943–45, see the State Department White
Paper, *United States Relations with China* (1949), Annex 47, pp. 564–76
(memoranda by U.S. Foreign Service Officers in China).

represented the defeat of counter-revolution—Fascist in Europe, militarist in Japan. Beneath the national rivalries was an undercurrent of ideological conflict. Whereas resistance movements tended to be Left-wing in character, collaborators were predominantly of the Right.[1] The end of the war saw in most Western countries a remarkable upsurge of pro-left feeling. Communism for the first and last time was almost respectable, admiration for Russian victories and achievements near universal.[2] In this prevailing mood most people were inclined to forget that a great ideological gulf still existed in the world.

The effect was seen in the widespread belief that a new world order could be established. The hardships and sacrifices of the war had been made bearable by visions of a bright future, in the building of which, it was assumed, all who had fought Fascism would join. These expectations were not confined to a credulous public. The Charter of the United Nations was itself drawn up on the principle that the anti-Fascist alliance would continue to ensure universal peace. Thus the war closed in high hopes that whatever was left of Fascism would soon be swept away and that the Western and Soviet worlds would remain in that state of amity and co-operation which a common struggle and victory had apparently brought to pass. Indeed, the writer recollects hoping and half-expecting that the Franco régime would be overthrown by the triumphant allies. Nor was this

---

[1] This was strikingly so in France. Although some Left-wing propagandists —e.g. 'Gracchus' (T. H. Wintringham) in *Your M.P.*, published 1944— alleged that there were Vichyist tendencies on the British Right, Britain was exceptional in that national considerations almost entirely overrode the ideological. Had there been a large Communist Party in Britain, there might have been a move on the Right to compromise with Hitler. In Nationalist China, however, the ideological conflict had come to overshadow the national. The result was ludicrous in a country supposedly fighting the common enemy as one of the 'Big Four' allies. Sometimes the Nationalist authorities allowed masses of their own troops to surrender to the Japanese so that they could be employed against the Communists at enemy expense (*The Times*, leader, 4 September 1945). Buying ammunition from the Japanese was also frequently resorted to (*Manchester Guardian* quoting the Nationalist general Ho Shu-yuan, Governor of Shantung, 30 October 1945).

[2] 'Had the Moscow Government accepted the British invitation to send representatives of their services to the Victory Parade, the Soviet contingent would probably have received a greater ovation from the London crowds than that accorded to any other military unit.' Kenneth Ingram, *The Cold War*, p. 10.

remarkable at the time.[1] It is true that in Britain such enthusiasm and optimism, although widespread, were not shared by everyone. Conservative suspicion of Soviet Russia, less vocal though it had become, had scarcely diminished during the years 1941–45, and those who had experience of Soviet aims and methods, in general viewed with concern the long reach of Moscow into central Europe. Nevertheless, as by-elections and still more the General Election showed, Conservative influence at the end of the war was low and still ebbing, and experience had not yet taught the mass of a Leftward-swinging electorate that the rearrangement of power produced by the war would completely change the attitude of the Soviet Union towards the Western democracies—or rather would reveal what its fundamental attitude had always been.

Thus it was that the eruption of Communist or near-Communist movements in different parts of the world was not yet regarded as an alarming occurrence by the bulk of the people. Indeed, there were those on the Left who took a more positive attitude. Did not they all have a common interest in eliminating 'reaction', without whose overthrow it would be impossible to establish a new world order in which imperialistic rivalries would have no place? If this should seem a reversion to the Popular Front tendencies of the 1930s, it should be remembered that few as yet realized that in the absence of an overwhelming Fascist threat a Popular Front was meaningless. True, the Labour Party had no desire to collaborate with the British Communists and repulsed all approaches made from that quarter, yet it was possible for Bevin when he took office as Foreign Secretary to believe that a Labour Government would get on better with Moscow than would a Conservative.[2]

Illusions such as these—far more prevalent amongst the Labour laity—reflect an attitude which was largely responsible for the intense opposition aroused by Western action taken

---

[1] As late as December 1946 the reaction to Fascism was still strong enough for the United Nations General Assembly to recommend not only withdrawal of ambassadors from Spain, but action by the Security Council unless there was a change of government within a reasonable time. As a result the British ambassador was withdrawn, but the recommendation failed to be reaffirmed in 1947.

[2] Lord Attlee interviewed by Francis Williams. *Listener*, 22 January 1959, p. 155.

against native Communist movements, whether by the British in putting down the rising in Athens in 1944, or by the Americans in assisting Chiang Kai-shek to gain control of all China.[1]

The year 1946 saw both a marked worsening of relations between Russia and the Western powers, and the political education of not a few. Hopes and illusions were soon dispersed by the brutal realism of Stalin's policy, and the immense amount of good-will which the Soviet Union had acquired in the West was rapidly forfeited. Indeed, the Soviet and satellite régimes were more and more becoming objects of distrust and obloquy. The reputation of Yenan, however, was as yet not much affected by this reaction against Communism.

When the first Western correspondents to visit the area reported on what they found, they were first of all impressed by the tolerance, popularity, and enthusiasm of the régime. All sections of the community had a say in the running of affairs, and the land, far from being collectivized, had been given to the peasants. Here was none of the grimness which was still in some measure associated with the rule of the Kremlin; rather did Mao Tse-tung and his followers seem to have all the peasant idealism and outlaw camaraderie of Robin Hood and his men.[2] Not surprisingly, therefore, we frequently find such comments as these made about the Yenan movement in the first post-war years:

The Yenan system is not Communism; it resembles an agrarian democracy.
                              The Times, leader, 25 January 1945

[1] In the case of Greece, although there were Labour ministers, including Bevin, in the British cabinet at the time, it is clear from his War Memoirs that the policy was primarily Churchill's. Much rank-and-file Labour opinion was inflamed. Churchill writes: 'In the House of Commons there was a great stir. I accepted willingly the challenge flung at us in an amendment moved by Sir Richard Acland . . . supported by Mr. Shinwell and Mr. Aneurin Bevan. There was a strong current of vague opinion, and even passion, of which these and other similar figures felt themselves the exponents.' See: Sir Winston Churchill, *Triumph and Tragedy*, pp. 251–5.

[2] To judge by the contrast he drew between Chungking and Yenan, one could be forgiven for thinking that the American correspondent Gunther Stein had wandered from the Court of King John into Sherwood Forest. See his eulogistic despatches to the *News Chronicle*, 2, 3, 30 January and 22 February 1945.

Communism in China now means nothing more or less than agrarian reform. . . .

Yorkshire Post, leader, 17 November 1945

The deadlock between Kuomintang and Communists is better appreciated if it is realised that Communism is but the modern name for China's oldest problem—the grievances of peasant against landlord.

Yorkshire Post, article by O. M. Green, 19 December 1945

In a memorandum he wrote on 9 December 1945, James Byrnes, the American Secretary of State, spoke of the 'so-called Communists' of China.[1] Nor was this an isolated use of the phrase:

The so-called Communist movement in China might rather be described as 'Socialist-Agrarian', though it contains a Communist element.

The Times, Military Correspondent, 6 November 1945

Hence the spread of the so-called Communist movement. 'So-called' because it is neither of the things which the name usually implies. It is not especially pro-Russian, and the Russians in the recent treaty with Chiang Kai-shek ignored it. Nor is it socialist so much as peasant in outlook.

Sunday Times, article by 'Scrutator', 6 January 1946

Much of this was true, but only superficially. The disarming idea that the Yenan movement could not be genuinely Communist because on the one hand it was a peasant movement and on the other had no apparent connexion with Moscow, needs to be examined further.

Revolutionary Communism as a political system differs from Western democracy in two important respects. First, the leadership is all-important, the opinions of the masses at most having a mere delaying effect until they can be re-moulded. Secondly, present policy is always governed by the ultimate objective; it is tactical and should never be mistaken for anything else.[2]

Failure to realize this was responsible for the false impressions about Chinese Communism current during the period 1945–50. If it was not clear whether Yenan was an orthodox Communist régime, the question should have been settled by a glance at the

---

[1] *United States Relations with China* (1949), p. 606.

[2] Lenin once justified a change of policy by remarking that a mountaineer faced with an insuperable obstacle will come down in order to find a better way up.

speeches, pronouncements, and claims of its leadership. Although it was ignored or glossed over in some of the earlier and more naïve reports of Western correspondents, the fact that the Chinese Communist leadership was imbued with Marxist–Leninism must have been obvious to anyone who took a more than superficial interest in Chinese affairs. Indeed the Chinese Communists freely admitted that they were orthodox Marxists and that their party organization followed the Russian model. In England, however, the significance of this was not recognized as fully as it might have been. As a people, the English are usually empirical in their judgements. They have a native distrust of dogma which occasionally leads them to draw wildly wrong conclusions about those whose actions are determined and inspired by dogma. Thus the policies of Hitler in the later 1930s came as a rude shock to many. He was merely fulfilling the programme, founded upon his racial beliefs, which he had outlined in *Mein Kampf*, but that unique prospectus had been ignored or its ideas dismissed as far-fetched and impractical. In contrast, Hitler's at first comparatively reasonable demands and frequent promises were, until a late hour, widely accepted as proof of his essential moderation. Similarly with Communist China, the distribution of land to the peasants, the democratic councils, the toleration and free discussion, all of which smoothed the way to the conquest of the whole country, were thought to indicate the true character of the régime.

But perhaps a further explanation can be advanced for the currency of the view that the Chinese Communist revolution was primarily an agrarian reform movement. Although this idea was not, especially in the early stages, confined to the Left, it was the Left which was usually accused of holding and propagating it. Partly this was a generalization used in the party battle. A favourite allegation of Conservatives during these years was that Socialists were poor opponents of Communism, being too gullible, too politically innocent, too ready to believe the best of the Communist world and the worst of their own. This might justifiably have been said of many Socialists at the end of the war, but disillusionment was rapid. Soon only the 'fellow travelling' fringe continued to idealize the Soviet system in face of all the evidence. Generally speaking, however, Socialists differed from Conservatives in their reading of develop-

B

ments in China, and for this reason. A great revolution is usually a complex affair, a confusion of unrelated or divergent motives and interests temporarily pulled together by some impelling historical need. It will therefore be interpreted in various ways according to the sympathies, experience or mental habits of the observer. Carlyle saw the French Revolution as primarily a great act of historical justice, the punishment of a frivolous and effete society. But then Carlyle was a most unfrivolous person. In the same way Socialists have a political philosophy which encourages them to take a sociological rather than a conspiratorial view of major revolutions, to regard such upheavals as emanations of the myriad wills, demands and aspirations of the common people. Thus on the Left there was a proneness to emphasize that side of the Communist revolution which was concerned with immediate land reforms, to look at the body of the movement rather than the Marxist core, and to see the whole affair as a big and welcome step in the inevitable emancipation of Asia's peasant masses.

The other factor taken to be evidence of the non-Communist or pseudo-Communist character of the Yenan régime was the apparent lack of connexion with Moscow. During the years 1945–46 when Chinese Communism was an enigma to many Western observers, it was pointed out that Moscow had held suspiciously aloof. To begin with, no Soviet help had been forthcoming during the war, even though the Communists were reduced to fighting with captured and makeshift weapons and were desperately deficient in medical supplies. The Russians, it might be argued, had no such aid to spare, but when on 14 August 1945 Stalin signed a treaty of friendship and alliance with Chiang Kai-shek, it seemed, on the face of it, that he had no interest in Chinese Communism and was prepared to see it subdued by the recognized government of China. For some, as for 'Scrutator', this attitude of the Soviet Union appeared to confirm the idea that whatever they might call themselves, the Chinese of Yenan were certainly not Communist. To draw this conclusion, however, was to make the common mistake of seeing only the ideological and not the national interests involved.

The main effect of the agrarian–democrat fallacy was to confuse Western opinion about the Chinese Communists when

Communism elsewhere was becoming hated and feared. The dream that the anti-Fascist concord would be preserved barely survived the war, and those social democrats who still had hopes of a Popular Front were speedily disillusioned by the fate of social democracy in Eastern Europe. Yet the reputation of the Chinese Communists for being benevolent reformers with whom it would be easy to co-operate continued to influence opinion until the régime, secure in its ascendancy over the Nationalists, began to show itself in a different light.

On 25 December 1947, Mao Tse-tung declared in the report he delivered to the Chinese Communist Party:

All the anti-imperialist forces of the various Eastern countries should also unite to oppose the oppression of imperialism and the reactionaries in their countries, and set as the goal of their struggle the liberation of the more than one thousand million oppressed people of the East.

We can completely conquer all obstacles and difficulties—our strength will be inevitable—but only if we are able to grasp the science of Marxist-Leninism. . . . This is the historic era in which world capitalism and imperialism are moving towards their doom, while world socialism and democracy are moving towards victory. The light of dawn is just ahead. We must be up and doing.[1]

If there had remained any doubt as to the course Chinese foreign policy would take once the Communists had mastered the country, this speech should have disposed of it. More significant, perhaps, was their action the following year when, the Yugoslav–Cominform schism taking place, they strongly denounced Tito. Nevertheless, despite these and other indications that a Communist China would be hostile to the West, an important body of opinion continued to regard the rise to power of Communism in China as a welcome development.

In explanation of this we must look to the contrast between the administrative honesty and efficiency of the Communists and the unparalleled corruption of the Nationalist régime. For there is a persistent liberal and radical tradition in Britain that foreign governments should be judged on their merits and treated accordingly. Are they doing well by their own people? If so they deserve support. If, however, they are doing badly by them, they should be ostracized or even opposed. This

[1] *New China News Agency.*

philanthropic influence[1] may even in certain circumstances determine the course of foreign policy. Furthermore, it can, and generally does, cut right across the policy of pure national interest, traditionally formulated in terms of power relationships, which is characteristic Tory policy. Fox's desire for an understanding with Napoleon, and Gladstone's feud with Disraeli over Turkey, are major historical instances. Moreover, the attitude of the philanthropists is generally governed not by absolute but by relative standards. To many Whigs and most radicals, the Napoleonic order, although not ideal, was at least preferable to the *ancien régime*. In the same way Gladstone would rather have had the Balkan peoples ruled by Imperial Russia than that they should continue the victims of Ottoman misgovernment. Often it is the dynamism of a régime which impresses. Until by his enormities Hitler put himself outside the bounds of civilized consideration, he was often praised for his public works and abolition of unemployment. Lloyd George returned from his visit to Germany in 1936 full of enthusiasm, and Mosley, originally a Socialist, was converted to Fascism largely because, in marked contrast to his experience as a minister under Ramsay MacDonald, he saw that under Hitler things got done. Mussolini was admired for the same reason, and was praised by Shaw. As for Soviet Communism, it is often urged, even by those who dislike it, that for the Russian people it is a great improvement upon what went before.[2] Thus, regardless of whether a foreign government is hostile, or represents an ideology alien to the British, there will always be those in Britain willing to speak up for it, if—as far as the welfare of its own people goes—it seems to be the better alternative.[3]

[1] In the case of China it took concrete form in the China Campaign Committee which was founded to help the Chinese in their struggle with Japan and which later championed the cause of the Chinese Communists. See Appendix I.

[2] Totalitarian régimes often attract the upper or upper middle class bureaucrat-philanthropist—a uniquely British phenomenon. Sydney and Beatrice Webb, arch-bureaucrats both, became devotees of the Soviet system when they found it to be a bureaucrat's paradise. Florence Nightingale would doubtless have been equally enthusiastic had she survived to see it.

[3] One may guess that there would have been little radical anger over Eden's Suez venture if the canal had been nationalized not by Nasser but by Farouk.

Prevailing reactions on the Right were, with a few exceptions, precisely the opposite of those outlined above. Conservatives did not, in the main, share the East–West holiday mood which for a short while survived the war, and a philanthropy that welcomes a hostile government provided it betters the lot of its people forms no part of the Tory heritage. Moreover, in their assessment of what the Yenan régime really was, they tended to be suspicious and pessimistic, and were unmoved by its alleged popularity. That it called itself Communist was sufficient; it was, they could hardly doubt, thoroughly orthodox and a satellite of Moscow.[1]

The assumption, however, that Yenan had or would come under Soviet control, was as wide of the mark as the belief that it was an agrarian-democracy. Unlike the East European Communist parties, the Chinese of Yenan owed their success entirely to their own efforts. They had to solve a problem which the Europeans, including the Russians, had never had to face— the absence of an urban proletariat. Mao Tse-tung, himself a farmer's son, determined to make the peasantry the spearhead of revolution. Stalin remained sceptical; he had, in any case, no experience of handling peasants except crushing them. This difference of approach partly explains the lack of co-operation between Yenan and Moscow. But the chief reason was that Stalin had no intention, by assisting a movement over which he had no control, of departing from a policy which, he had decided, would best serve Soviet national interests. Russian

---

[1] Some Conservative opinion was influenced by the 'agrarian-democrat' idea, but only at the very beginning. Before long views such as these had become characteristic:

Walter Fletcher: 'It is right to analyse to some extent what the Northern Communist movement is. Undoubtedly at the centre of it and controlling the machine there is the pure dyed-in-the-wool, Kremlin-trained, toeing-the-line, Communist hard core.' [Laughter] H. C. Debs. Vol. 459. Col. 669 (9 December 1948).

Brigadier Fitzroy Maclean: 'We must face up to the fact that if China is allowed to go Communist she will become a Soviet dominion . . .' Ibid. Col. 658.

Daily Mail, leader: 'The fall of China is not only a triumph for the local Communists. It is the biggest victory Russia has won since the Allied defeat of Germany gave her the key to Eastern Europe.' (20 January 1949); 'Russian imperialism has long had its eye on China, and, as has happened elsewhere, Communism is merely its vehicle.' (21 January 1949).

policy in China at the end of the war was to support the Nationalists, for in this way Stalin could extort concessions from a weak China without arousing the opposition of the West. Much has been made, first of Stalin's supposed help to the Chinese Communists by his denying, in 1944–45 when the Americans were in a position to intervene decisively, that he had any interest in them or that they were even true Communists,[1] and secondly of the Russian transfer to them, in the course of the evacuation of Manchuria in 1946, of Japanese stores of arms. These two acts of neighbourly assistance, however, cost nothing. On the other hand, the Russians stripped Manchuria, an industrial province within the Communist sphere of influence, of all its plant and machinery, a move which caused embarrassment in Yenan.[2] What evidence there is shows that until the tide had turned decisively in the Communists' favour, Stalin's policy was dictated purely by Russian national interests.[3] On the Chinese side the Soviet Union was admired as a great pioneer of socialism from whom they had much to learn, but if the relationship was one of master and pupil, it was never one of master and puppet. Such an interpretation, which actually became official doctrine in the United States, may be compared to the Communist accusation that Britain was ruled from Washington, or even Wall Street. Whether believed or not by those who made it, it had the effect of creating a 'bogy' image in the war of ideological propaganda.

When we look at the tremendous repercussions produced in the West by the Czech *coup* of 1948, as well as at the excitement aroused by the Hungarian rising in 1956, the fall of China to Communism—an event of immeasurably greater significance— seems to have been accepted in Britain almost with equanimity. Largely, of course, this is to be explained by the nearness of the

[1] From conversations which Stalin and Molotov had with General Hurley (American Ambassador to China), Harry Hopkins (Truman's representative) and T. V. Soong (Chinese Premier and Foreign Minister). See: *United States Relations with China* (1949), pp. 72, 94–5, 115; H. Feis, *The China Tangle*, p. 319.

[2] See: article by Gerald Samson, who had shortly returned from China, *News Chronicle*, 27 January 1947; Otto B. van der Sprenkel, Robert Guillain and Michael Lindsay, *New China: Three Views*, p. 74.

[3] This is the conclusion of Isaac Deutscher. *Stalin: A Political Biography*, p. 529.

former and the remoteness of the latter, as well as by the radical acceptance of emergent Asia already discussed. But was there another reason? Why was it that Conservative and business opinion, although recognizing the rise of Communism in China as a danger, seemed little inclined to support the attempts made by the United States to dam the tide? The answer seems to lie in the suspicion which existed of American aims.

When Japan collapsed it was the United States which succeeded as the leading power in the Far East, her contribution to the enemy's defeat having been immensely greater than that of the other allies. This newly won paramountcy the American leaders were resolved to preserve. With the end of the European war in sight, Britain was free to play an increasing part in the struggle against Japan, but her participation was not wholly welcomed in Washington, and by some was regarded as an unwanted intrusion into what was considered to be an exclusively American theatre of operations.[1] In the American view, there could be no return to European colonialism in eastern Asia. Roosevelt was determined that Indo-China should not go back to France and that the Dutch East Indies should have self-government. Hong Kong, he thought, should be returned to the Chinese.[2] In place of the rival imperialisms of Japan and the European powers, there was to be established a beneficent partnership between Nanking and Washington. China, under American guidance and developed by American capital was to become a great power and stabilizing force in the new Asia.[3]

These new arrangements were not welcomed by the European colonial and trading nations. Britain, in particular, had a large and traditional interest in the commerce of China. When, after granting facilities to American business men, the Kuomintang Government refused to open its ports to British ships, failed to

[1] When, in September 1944, Churchill proposed sending strong British air and naval forces into the central Pacific, his offer was accepted by Roosevelt, but the American Chiefs of Staff were unenthusiastic, and one, Admiral King, was undisguisedly hostile. See: Chester Wilmot, *Struggle for Europe*, pp. 641–2.

[2] Ibid., p. 653.

[3] Harold M. Vinacke, *The United States and the Far East, 1945–1951*, pp. 23–4.

restore British property on the Yangtze, and delayed resuming payments on British loans,[1] fears which had already been expressed in Parliament and the press that the United States was bent upon creating an exclusive economic empire in China appeared to be confirmed.[2] Thus, from the commercial point of view, the establishment of an efficient Chinese government with whom it would be possible to trade, even though that government should be Communist, seemed to British merchants preferable to a situation from which they benefited little.

There was, however, small likelihood that the United States could turn China into a vast monopoly market, even had the Kuomintang survived. Xenophobia, poverty and a corrupt bureaucracy would have made the country extraordinarily difficult to exploit. The British attitude really illustrates a touchiness which was characteristic of the time, and for which a changed status in the world, particularly in relation to the Americans, whose treatment of the British was often remarkable for its tactlessness, was in large part responsible.[3]

So far we have examined opinions reflected in the nation generally or amongst important elements of it. We shall now consider the views of a few individuals whose special knowledge, experience or position entitles them to our notice.

The first Lord Lindsay of Birker, Master of Balliol until 1949 and a Labour peer from 1945, raised the subject of China several times in the House of Lords between 1946 and 1948. Basing his arguments upon the first-hand knowledge of his son, Michael, who had resided in China throughout the war, he constituted himself as the leading Parliamentary critic of United States policy.

[1] Article by O. M. Green quoting Lord Ammon, leader of a Parliamentary Mission, and Sir Ralph Stevenson, the British Ambassador to China. *Observer*, 26 October 1947.

[2] See: James Callaghan. H.C. Debs. Vol. 417. Cols. 750–1 (13 December 1945); D. Rees-Williams. Ibid. Vol. 437. Cols. 1908–9 (16 May 1947); an article by George Johnston, *Daily Mail*, 27 September 1945; *New Statesman*, 23 November 1946. There were other and later references of a similar character.

[3] Suspicion was not one-sided. General Hurley, American Ambassador to China 1944–5, thought that the British were supporting the Chinese Communists at that time (see Herbert Feis, *The China Tangle*, pp. 410–1). Similar allegations were made in an article by Christopher Rand in the *New York Herald Tribune*, 16 January 1948.

He first spoke on the subject in July 1946, making the point that the Chinese Communists had a popular, in many ways democratic government, whereas the Kuomintang was a dictatorship possessing concentration camps and a Gestapo and employing troops who had previously fought for the Japanese. It was therefore wrong, he maintained, for the Americans, with the British behind them, to support the Kuomintang against the Communists.[1] Six months later, in January 1947, Lord Lindsay raised the matter again by sponsoring a debate devoted entirely to the situation in China. By then General Marshall's mission of mediation had failed and the Nationalists appeared at last to be gaining the advantage. This time he stressed the danger of Russian intervention and advocated consultations between the three great powers. It would be intolerable, he concluded, if Britain acquiesced in the destruction of 'an honest and sincere agrarian community' by a government compared with which the Franco régime seemed liberal.[2] Later, in June 1947, he deplored the continuance of the civil war claiming that but for American assistance to the Nationalists, who believed that the United States would never allow them to be defeated, it would end in six months.[3] When, the following year, it was fairly clear that the Communists would triumph, Lord Lindsay advocated both seeking an arrangement with them and cutting off aid to the Nationalists, otherwise 'there is no hope of finding that the new victorious Government will be at least friendly to this country'.[4]

Lord Lindsay thus appears as a characteristic radical idealist with all the virtues and weaknesses of one looking at affairs from that particular standpoint. Although greatly concerned with the welfare of the people of China and the danger that the Chinese civil war would involve the great powers, he showed no real appreciation of what Chinese Communism was or would lead to. Eventually his views changed, as is shown by his open letter to Mao Tse-tung published early in 1951. He wrote:

The high hopes which we had in earlier days of the results of your Government coming to full power and the bitter disappointment

[1] H.L. Debs. Vol. 142. Cols. 1074–5 (29 July 1946).
[2] Ibid. Vol. 145. Cols. 110–24 (23 January 1947).
[3] Ibid. Vol. 148. Cols. 522–4 (11 June 1947).
[4] Ibid. Vol. 154. Cols. 375–8 (3 March 1948).

and disillusionment which the recent announcements and actions of your Government have produced in people like myself make me bold to address you and to pray you to return to the way of negotiation for the settlement of differences between our countries; to deal with the United Nations on the basis of the facts and to follow out your own principles against doctrinairism and authoritarianism.[1]

When Lord Lindsay died a year later, it was said of him:

He shared with his friend, Archbishop Temple, a natural interest in ordinary men and women and his belief in their capacity for good. He certainly believed in their capacity to govern themselves wisely.[2]

His son, Michael Lindsay, a student of politics, lectured at the University of Peking from 1938 to 1941, acted as press attaché to the British embassy in Chungking in 1940, and during the last years of the war served with the Yenan Communists. He also married a Chinese lady. Inasmuch as his experience of the situation in China as it stood at the end of the war could be rivalled by few other Westerners, his views were not lightly to be dismissed. During the years under discussion his usual line of argument was that if the Chinese Communists showed signs of becoming extremist or moving closer to Russia, Western and particularly American policy was to blame.[3] Early in 1959 Lord Lindsay (as he now was) allowed the writer to question him on his views. The following is not a verbatim record but represents accurately the sense of question and answer:

B.E.P.: You say in your book *China and the Cold War* that the Chinese Communists have changed since you were in Yenan in 1945. Is this a fundamental or a superficial change? In other words, was their war-time liberalism genuine or tactical?

Lord L.: I had grounds for thinking that the Chinese Communists might continue to be liberal. The whole atmosphere in Yenan during the war was more liberal. And then Mao had made a number of statements, which, if made today, would almost certainly convict him of Rightism.

B.E.P.: So you worked for better relations between Britain and the Chinese Communists during 1946–47, and this is reflected in your father's speeches?

[1] Extract from a letter published in the *Manchester Guardian*, 7 February 1951.   [2] George Wigg, M.P., *The Times*, 31 March 1952.

[3] See, for example, letters to *The Times*, 5 April 1948 and 25 January 1949, and the article in the *Sunday Times*, 4 December 1949.

Lord L.: Yes.

B.E.P.: But if Mao and his colleagues were avowed Marxist–
Leninists, how could their attitude towards the West be anything
other than hostile?

Lord L.: Well, not necessarily. People don't often realize that Marx-
ism is a curious mixture in which there are liberal elements. For
example, Engels said that the first condition of freedom was that
all officials should be responsible for their actions to every citizen,
before the ordinary courts and according to the common law.
The Chinese, while remaining Marxists, were not bound to go
the way of Stalin. Anyway, I gave them the benefit of the doubt
and thought it worth trying to improve relations. They heard
nothing except the Russian line on events in the outside world.
Had we sent representatives to Yenan, and told them what the
Russians were really up to in Europe, this might have had some
influence on their future course. At least by doing so we could
have tested their sincerity.

B.E.P.: Was there any point when you finally despaired of them?

Lord L.: Yes. When they sent the Liu Ning-i delegation to Britain
in 1950. *Tribune* called it the rudest delegation ever to have come
to this country.

Michael Lindsay saw in Chinese Communism two opposing
tendencies:

on the one hand, rational thought, good administration and respect
for the common man; on the other, unreasoning faith in dogma,
bureaucracy and contempt for the individual. To an outside observer
this conflict seems very fundamental; the development of China is
likely to take completely different paths according to which tendency predominates.[1]

It was his conviction that the West should have done its utmost
to see that the former prevailed.

The same view was taken by another sinologist, the former
consul and Foreign Office expert on the Far East, Sir John
Pratt. In March 1950 he wrote:

The deepest cleavage, however, is not regional but in the realm of
ideas—the cleavage between the ideas of Mao Tse-tung and Chou
En-lai on the one hand, whose Communism derives as much from
the Confucian dialectic as from Marx, and those of Li Li-san and
Liu Shih-chi on the other hand, the fanatical doctrinaires who

[1] Otto B. van der Sprenkel, Robert Guillain and Michael Lindsay, *New
China: Three Views*, pp. 130–1.

would sacrifice even China's independence on the altar of Marxist–Leninist theory. If American policy had been less inept (to use no stronger word) the doctrinaires would have very little influence in China to-day.[1]

It is impossible to say now whether a more favourable policy pursued by the United States and Britain towards the Chinese Communists in the years before they assumed power would have made much difference to relations with them after. But it hardly seems likely. Sir John Pratt, in speaking of the Chinese heritage, has stated that Mao's aim may well be to re-establish the Middle Kingdom surrounded by satellite states looking up to her as the fountainhead of civilization.[2] Whether the dynamism of the Chinese revolution is dogmatically Communist or traditionally nationalist in character makes little difference; there would be bound to be a collision with those Western powers whose interests have impinged upon China at so many points and until recently in so unequal a fashion.

The views of G. F. Hudson are interesting because they are in complete contrast to those just quoted. An Oxford historian and expert on the Orient, he saddled the blame for the Nationalist débâcle largely upon American policy:

Several factors conducive to a reactionary trend existed in the Kuomintang at the end of the war with Japan, but none contributed so much to the liquidation of the liberal movement as the illusions about the Chinese Communists on which American policy was based. By the time the American Government had got round to the realization that forcing a partnership with Communists on a friendly, allied government was not the wisest of all possible policies, it was too late either to save the Kuomintang or to liberalize it.[3]

Again, he claimed that the Chinese Nationalist army 'the fighting spirit of which had been good enough in the autumn of 1945' (!) was deprived of whatever chance it had of winning in 1946 by General Marshall's 'futile mission'.[4] All this is highly debatable. Indeed, bearing in mind the weakness and corruption exhibited by the Kuomintang even before the end of the

---

[1] *Manchester Guardian*, 14 March 1950.
[2] Ibid.
[3] G. F. Hudson, *Questions of East and West*, p. 115. This book is a collection of articles published chiefly in the *Nineteenth Century and After* (from 1951, the *Twentieth Century*).   [4] Ibid., p. 153.

war, it would seem more probable that but for American aid and attempts at mediation, the end would have come sooner. Nationalist China collapsed because everyone had lost faith in it including its leaders. Had the Kuomintang possessed the slightest capacity it would have commenced an administrative overhaul without waiting for the subjugation of the Communists.

These conclusions about the Chinese revolution, however, are but one aspect of a more general thesis. Hudson dismisses the view that the rising masses of Asia can be won over to a liberal, democratic way of life:

It is time for Western liberals to take stock of the situation with a more realistic view of the short-term prospects of democracy outside the relatively small part of the world where it is well rooted. They have been so given to projecting their own ideals upon distant peoples, and so accustomed to expecting the victorious advance of liberal principles over the world, that they are unable to recognize the non-conforming reality. . . . history keeps showing them, not a triumphal progress of fraternal, democratic nations into the Century of the Common Man, but new marches of Xerxes to subdue Hellas . . .[1]

There is much here that is true. Most attempts to graft Western democratic systems and standards upon non-European societies have failed, and in contemporary Asia and Africa, shallow-rooted constitutional government has tended increasingly to give way to military rule. What may be questioned, however, is the assumption that the West must set its face against xeno-phobic nationalism rather than seek to redress the social, economic and psychological factors that have produced it. Hudson advocates, in effect, discipline—

Western statesmen . . . cannot afford to be too tolerant of the in-fantile destructiveness of newborn democracies; they may even have to face the political necessity of supporting regimes of which in other circumstances they would strongly disapprove.[2]

rather than charity—

One of the conditions of a successful policy . . . is a . . . rejection of the wishful illusion which has already wrought such disaster, that well-meaning but blind support of popular 'upsurges of the masses' and

[1] Ibid., pp. 111–12.   [2] Ibid., pp. 114–15.

generous economic handouts will of themselves magically stem the march of the new conquerors.[1]

Yet as recent developments in Cuba have shown, it is just such a response as this by the West which enables Communism to cash in upon nationalism.

For all his expertise and forceful reasoning, it would seem that Hudson's view of the world is coloured by an outlook common to certain English intellectuals: those for whom civilization—by which they mean their own cultivated classical heritage—must be preserved at all costs. One such was Dean Inge. Another was Gilbert Murray, who in his last days was also preoccupied with 'new marches of Xerxes', and of whom Arnold Toynbee wrote:

[His classical] outlook made him sometimes feel dubious about the struggles of non-western peoples to shake off western domination. Here his love of liberty had to contend with his concern for civilization. In his view, the torch-bearer of civilization in our time was the West, and he was afraid that the flickering flame might be extinguished by inexperienced hands. At the time of the invasion of Egypt last year he publicly dissociated himself from the critics of Sir Anthony Eden.[2]

It may well be doubted whether coercive policies derived from such an outlook are ultimately realistic, yet, in a country where over-anxiety to see things from the foreigner's point of view is almost a national complaint, the sombre observations of the classical rearguard may on occasion prove salutary.

In fine, opinion about the nature and rise of Chinese Communism during the years 1945–49 was marked by great diversity, but the main trends are clear. In 1945–46 the weight of opinion was undoubtedly favourable to the Chinese Communists. This is attributable partly to the world-wide ideological shift which underlay the Second World War, partly to the prevailing optimism with which the war ended, and partly to some mistaken ideas about Chinese Communism itself. The Cold War proved to be an education in political realism, yet

[1] Ibid., p. 118.
[2] 'Reminiscences of Gilbert Murray', article in the *Listener*, 22 August 1957. For Murray's views on Suez, see his article in the *Sunday Times*, 16 December 1956, entitled 'The Shadow of Barbarism'.

the Yenan régime continued to excite hopes and expectations, even amongst those who knew it best. It seems strange that the instinctive, sceptical Tory reaction to Chinese Communism should have proved in the end to be better justified than the assessments of such first-hand observers as Michael Lindsay. The Sinophiles and radicals were unduly swayed by their enthusiasm for an emergent China: Chinese Communism might be a puzzle, its leaders enigmatic, its methods uncharacteristic, its objects unknown, but because it brought hope to a wretched people, they put their doubts aside and spoke up for it. Tories, on the other hand, with few exceptions, were at best unconcerned with, at worst hostile to, the growth of Asian nationalism. In China they simply saw a vast shift in the world balance of power—in the words of Churchill 'the worst disaster suffered by the West since the war'[1]—yet could not bring themselves to support American policy, being critical of its methods and jealous of certain of its objectives.

What bearing had opinion upon policy? Throughout the civil war British policy towards China consisted merely of waiting until matters sorted themselves out. This may seem a reasonable, natural course to have followed, yet if for a moment we take a Toynbeean, world-historical view of these events, we might feel justified in asking why Chinese Communism was not strangled in its cradle—a fate which Russian Communism only narrowly escaped. China's natural resources, though undeveloped, were known to be vast. Her population approached a quarter of the globe's. If she fell to Communism, would not this tip the balance of world power finally in favour of the East, even though the full effects might not be felt for many years? Yet in 1945–46 the Western powers might have countered this threat by throwing into China their splendidly equipped and experienced armies backed by a degree of war production never previously attained. In the last resort the Soviet Union would have been powerless to interfere. She had emerged from the war victorious but weakened, having suffered enormous casualties and great devastation. Above all she possessed neither the atomic bomb nor the immense air strength of the West. This brief combination of circumstances, of Western might, Russian exhaustion, and Chinese Communism's inability as yet to play more than a

[1] Speech at Boston, 31 March 1949. *The Times*, 1 April 1949.

local role, must be accounted as providing one of the great last chances of history, comparable perhaps with the opportunity temporarily presented to Carthage after Cannae of reinforcing Hannibal and crushing Rome. By striking then, the West might have saved China from Communism, and perhaps even have overthrown the Russian and European Communist régimes. But the opportunity faded, and by 1949, when the Soviet Union exploded her first atomic bomb and the Chinese Communists swiftly seized control of all China, the chance had gone never to recur.

To talk of chance and opportunity, however, is tantamount to assuming that the American and British Governments had the freedom of action of a Frederick or Napoleon. There was, of course, no real likelihood that such developments would ensue, for apart from the mood of relaxation that victory after a long and hard-fought conflict inevitably brings, Western opinion—which not only restrains but to a large extent is reflected in Western governments—would have regarded military intervention on the required scale at best as reckless and burdensome, at worst as monstrously immoral.[1] Indeed, undisguised aggressive war is now regarded with such abhorrence that it is doubtful whether in the Western world it can any longer be regarded as a practical instrument of policy. Suez was the last occasion on which it was tried, and the reactions provoked by that exploit were not of the sort to encourage a repetition. Moreover, even when war is forced upon them, Western countries, and perhaps Britain in particular, have generally shown in the early stages a reluctance to employ more force than the immediate situation demands, and sometimes not even that.[2]

---

[1] 'It would have been folly, and it would be folly today, to attempt to impose our way of life on these huge areas [i.e. Russia and China] by force! In 1945 and 1946, of all years, such thoughts would have been rejected by the American people before they were even expressed. That was the time when Congressmen in Washington joined in the call to "get the boys back home", and our influence throughout the world, as well as China, waned as the millions of American soldiers were processed through the discharge centers.' Harry S. Truman, *Years of Trial and Hope 1946–1953*, p. 96.

[2] The British and French commenced the Second World War full of inhibitions. During the first few months, for example, the R.A.F. was forbidden to bomb enemy towns except with leaflets; it took German and Japanese ruthlessness to goad the Allies into waging total war. The Korean

In short, the Western democracies were psychologically unfitted to undertake the suppression of a strong, popular movement with which they had no overt quarrel merely on the grounds that it presented a possible future threat. Marshall's efforts to make peace and bring the Communists into a coalition met with almost universal acclaim in Britain, whereas the possibility of Western military intervention was not even publicly discussed.[1]

But beyond this point British and American opinion diverged. American hopes and plans were centred upon the Nationalists. Even when General Marshall was attempting to arrange a settlement, American energies were directed to the arming, supplying and financing of the forces of Chiang Kai-shek. There was little chance of Anglo-American co-operation here. In Britain the realists held that to shore up the Kuomintang was a foolish misdirection of effort; the radical idealists regarded such support as being morally inexcusable—as Gladstone had done the preservation of the Ottoman Empire.[2]

Naturally, to talk of the British view and the American view is to over-simplify. Some Conservative opinion was in sympathy with the American approach to the problem. The American Government, on the other hand, was not so naïve in its attitude towards Nationalist China as its policy would lead the superficial observer to think. The important White Paper on United States relations with China published in August 1949 shows how very far from being deluded the State Department was. Nevertheless, despite this overlapping, the centres of gravity of opinion

War was kept within geographical and non-nuclear bounds. At Suez it was claimed that every effort was made by British pilots to avoid killing or injuring Egyptian personnel, even in attacks upon aircraft.

[1] The writer has noted only one case of virtual advocacy of military intervention in China, and that significantly by a general. See the *Daily Telegraph*, article by Lt.-General H. G. Martin, 18 November 1948.

[2] The Eastern Question of the late 1870s and the Far Eastern Question of the late 1940s make an interesting parallel. Each arose because a great anti-Russian buffer state was in decay. Each involved pro-Russian nationalism. Each set off a controversy as to how the growing influence of Russia should be checked, whether by buttressing the old order or by accepting and encouraging the nationalism of the new. In the later crisis and its aftermath, the American Government incurred much the same odium amongst British radicals as Disraeli had in the earlier.

c

in both countries were well apart, and it was largely because of this that the policies, of London and Washington which after the failure of the Marshall Mission might usefully have come together, went instead their separate and futile ways.

II

The Recognition Question

The recognition of a change in the international landscape—a new régime, a conquest or annexation, the birth or extinction of a state—has increasingly become a subject of more than professional concern. Indeed, when nationalism or ideological rivalries are involved it is often a matter of decided opinions and occasionally arouses passions too strong for governments to ignore. Rarely has the recognition of a new régime set off as much controversy as in the case of Communist China. The question was one upon which Western opinion came to be sharply divided. In Britain it led to a dispute between the parties; in the United States it indulged the national passion for moral censure; and between the two countries it at length caused a contention in which conflicting interests, traditions and sentiments all played a part.

To add confusion to a complicated issue, different ideas prevail as to what recognition is or what it implies. The traditional British view, subscribed to by most leading political figures, is that it is no more than the formal acknowledgement of a new situation, and in the case of a new government, the initial step in establishing relations. Whether the change to be recognized is welcome or unwelcome is irrelevant. Speaking in the House of Commons on 17 November 1949, Churchill declared:

Recognizing a person is not necessarily an act of approval. . . . One has to recognize lots of things and people in this world of sin and woe that one does not like. The reason for having diplomatic relations is not to confer a compliment but to secure a convenience.[1]

On 24 May following, both Bevin and Eden also stated that recognition of a government should not depend upon its political colour.[2]

British practice in this matter has not been without its critics, for there is a persistent assumption that if it does not signify

[1] H.C. Debs. Vol. 469. Col. 2225.
[2] Ibid. Vol. 475. Cols. 2081–2, 2071.

approval, recognition at least implies acceptance, giving a new régime an international standing it might otherwise lack. Indeed, there are some for whom recognition of a régime of bad character must be considered an immoral act, and the government responsible as much dishonoured by the proceeding as a man in public office who knowingly does business with a rogue. The political and economic needs which have dictated the step, even when these are known, rarely weigh as much with those not having to make the decision as considerations of principle. Hence recognition is liable to excite high feeling, especially if it appears to condone the activities or even the existence of somebody's ideological *bête noire*. In the late 1930s much Left-wing resentment was caused in Britain by the National Government's recognition of Franco Spain and the Italian annexation of Abyssinia. It was felt that for the sake of expediency a vital principle had been flouted. In the same way some Conservatives regarded the Labour Government's *de jure* recognition of Communist China early in 1950 as a moral lapse. This was not a very common reaction; fewer Tories than radicals are likely to attack a policy purely on moral grounds. But many on the Right regarded the recognition of Communist China as a disagreeable step which only imperative necessity or substantial advantages could justify.

This coolness to some extent characterized public opinion as a whole during the first months of the new régime's existence. According to a poll taken in November 1949, a majority of Labour voters as well as a much greater percentage of Tories were at that time hostile to recognition. The Liberals were equally divided.[1] In explanation it should be recalled that relations between Britain and the Chinese Communists had got off to a bad start. The previous April, British warships navigating the Yangtse had been fired upon by the Communist armies occupying the north bank, suffering, in consequence, heavy casualties and damage. Undoubtedly the fault lay partly with the British naval authorities who, in ordering the ships to sail between the two front lines on the eve of a Communist offensive, had acted either rashly or with a startling unawareness of what was happening in China. Yet if the incident itself was hardly surprising, the aftermath was significant. Their detention of the

[1] See Appendix III, A1.

frigate *Amethyst*, their offer to release her provided she assisted them in attacking the Nationalists, their intransigence in negotiation, their exploitation of the incident for purposes of propaganda, and finally their rage and abuse when after three months the *Amethyst* made her dramatic night escape to the sea —all this showed that in their relations with the West the Chinese Communists could be, and would probably continue to be, as uncompromising as Stalin. Nevertheless, during the latter half of 1949, and particularly after 1 October when the People's Republic of China was formally proclaimed in Peking, the need for recognition was urged from three influential quarters, although for differing reasons.

Radical opinion was keen to see friendly relations develop between Britain and the new China despite what had occurred.[1] For Liberals it was part of their internationalism; for Socialists a reflection of their belief in political, economic and social evolution. On 31 December 1949 the *New Statesman* characteristically observed:

[Mao Tse-tung's] triumph faces the Western democracies with the problem whether in this whole area Communism is not objectively a liberating force which may well provide the kind of authoritarian regime that in Western Europe was the immediate successor to feudalism and the necessary prelude to political democracy. Is it Communism we object to, or Russian domination of Communist regimes? Are we, as Socialists, to oppose social revolution and repress the uprising against White ascendancy?

This shows again how the radical outlook was based on a philanthropy governed by relative standards. It was not a question of whether a régime was good or bad, but whether it was moving in the right direction. If it was, much could be forgiven, much should be encouraged.

China [said the Lord Chancellor in December 1950], is both a young and an old country with a great history and great traditions. She has been through an ordeal and is emerging with the enthusiasm of youth. As a great nation she is now openly taking her place in the world. Surely we wish her well.[2]

---

[1] The *Manchester Guardian*, for example, regretted the parade of the *Amethyst*'s men through the streets of London in November, as a chauvinistic spectacle likely to prejudice the restoration of Anglo-Chinese friendship (5 November 1949).

[2] H.L. Debs. Vol. 169. Col. 1058 (14 December 1950).

When Lord Jowitt spoke these words, the forces of the United Nations, British included, had just been hurled back by a massive Chinese offensive in Korea. The same sentiments led some radicals to excuse political intolerance in Ghana by claiming that a new country must run the same sort of course as Britain did under the Stuarts, and Dr. Hewlett Johnson, the 'Red' Dean of Canterbury, to assert in justification of Stalinist oppression that early Christianity was often propagated by the same methods. Here, in fact, is the characteristic radical approach to education—a distrust of coercion and an emphasis upon the unhampered self-development of the individual—applied to the society of states.

Support, at least for the principle of recognition, also came from Churchill when, on 17 November 1949, he spoke on the subject in the House of Commons:

Now the question has arisen also of what our attitude should be towards the Chinese Communists who have gained control over so large a part of China. Ought we to recognise them or not?

After making the point that recognition was not a compliment, but for convenience, he went on:

When a large and powerful mass of people are organized together and are masters of an immense area and of great populations, it may be necessary to have relations with them. One may say that when relations are most difficult, that is the time when diplomacy is most needed.[1]

Although other Conservatives occasionally expressed similar opinions, none was of note, and for long they seem to have been a minority in the party. The view was much more a Socialist and Liberal one, as was apparent during the controversy over Communist China's claim to a seat in the United Nations. Indeed, after the Labour Government had recognized the People's Republic, Churchill's utterance on this occasion, when quoted in support of the policy they were so busily attacking, became almost an embarrassment to his followers. Unlike the radicals, however, he had little sympathy for the emergence of Asia. His intention may partly have been, as Leader of the Opposition, to insure himself against the Labour Government's claiming

[1] H.C. Debs. Vol. 469. Cols. 2225–6.

sole credit for recognition in the event of successful results, but more important than this, it was undoubtedly his mature conviction that as a general principle the centres of world power should be in touch with one another.

We ought certainly [he continued] to have suitable contacts with this large part of the world's surface and population under the control of the Chinese Communists. We ought to have them on general grounds. Again I say it seems difficult to justify having full diplomatic relations with the Soviet Government in Moscow and remaining without even *de facto* contacts with its enormous offshoots into China.[1]

This was characteristic. For Churchill was realist enough to regard ideology as the ultimate, but only the ultimate determinant of policy.

Thirdly there was the opinion of the City of London, especially those commercial and financial interests having business with the Far East.[2] Here the main concern was the future of Britain's trade with China and of the assets possessed there. The latter, representing a century of investment and trading activity, had grown to exceed those of any other power. Despite war losses of some £14 million, the value of physical properties alone, not counting shipping or assets in Hong Kong, was thought to total about £110 million in 1945.[3] The Communists now had all this within their grasp. They refused any approach at the commercial level.[4] With diplomatic contact it might be possible to convince Peking of the advantages of continued trade and save British firms from local exactions. If the Chinese were resolved to nationalize, an ambassador's representations might ensure a measure of compensation. Moreover, Chiang Kai-shek's blockade was damaging British commerce and a general withdrawal of support from the Nationalists could help to bring this annoyance to an end. Although the recognition of the Communists might achieve none of these results, at least it

---

[1] Ibid. Col. 2226.   [2] See Appendix I, The China Association.
[3] H.C. Debs. Vol. 475. Cols. 6–7. This estimate, to which should be added £53 million to represent Chinese Government and Railway Bonds, was probably too low. A later official estimate put the total value of British assets in China as something between £200 million and £250 million. See Eden, H.C. Debs. Vol. 501. Col. 267 (20 May 1952).
[4] *Survey of International Affairs, 1949–50*, p. 335.

offered a chance. Failure to recognize would almost certainly bring disruption and loss.

By the end of 1949 opinion was more favourable towards recognition than it had been earlier. Even the Conservative press agreed that Britain could ill afford to lack relations with the masters of China. But recognition was one thing, the decision to recognize another. Before the decision could be made, all the possible repercussions, domestic as well as international, would have to be considered and weighed. Recognition might have its advantages, but when and in what circumstances should the step be taken?

Conservative opinion was convinced that it would be bad for Britain to act alone, and above all to do so independently of the United States. Churchill, despite his powerful advocacy of recognition, was careful to make this clear.[1] Concern about keeping in step with Washington was particularly marked amongst Conservatives at the time. They saw themselves as the watchdogs of the American alliance. Was the Labour Party wholehearted over it? The Government might be, and no one, they agreed, had done more than the Foreign Secretary to ensure that the United States was committed to the defence and economic recovery of Western Europe, but towards the Left were wilder spirits, men for whom dependence upon the leading capitalist power was the betrayal of a faith, who hankered after a Third Force, and who wished to see Britain play a role in the world more like that of Nehru's India. Whether or not many Conservatives really believed that the tip of the Labour tail would ever wag body and head, it suited them to say that it might.[2] It suited them too, amid the prevailing grey of Socialist Britain, to point westward where the land was bright. This attraction of America for the British Right must be seen in its context, for although usual it is not immutable. Indeed, at the time of the Suez intervention there was an upsurge of Tory hostility towards the United States which was surprising in its

---

[1] H.C. Debs. Vol. 469. Col. 2226 (17 November 1949).

[2] On one occasion, fully seventy Labour members abstained from supporting the Government in a foreign affairs debate, a gesture denounced by Bevin as 'a stab in the back'. The phrase became famous, and from then on the Right-wing cartoonist Cummings usually depicted the Foreign Secretary with a dagger in his back.

suddenness and bitterness. But this is a reaction likely to occur only when the Americans are jolted into remembering that they too have a radical tradition and act accordingly. In 1949 there was little likelihood of this. The cold war was becoming more intense and effectively overshadowed those aspects of imperialism so upsetting to American susceptibilities. The great European retreat from Asia had removed a major grievance, and the attempt to suppress armed Communism in the few colonies which remained allayed a minor one. Moreover, in 1949 Churchill was head of the Conservative Party, and while he remained so, the overriding importance of the American connexion was kept firmly before the Tory mind.[1]

In effect, however, the Opposition was not merely demanding that Britain and the United States should recognize at the same time; it was acquiescing in a departure from traditional British practice. For American practice differs from British in a way which made it unlikely that the United States would recognize Communist China until long after all benefit to Britain would be lost.

Recognition is a political act, conferred or withheld in accordance with the government's ideas of what the national interest requires, although within the range of what is politically practicable. But what does the national interest require? In the answer to this question lies the real difference between British and American practice on recognition, apparent at least since the early years of the century. In 1913 Grey had felt obliged to recognize the notorious Huerta régime of Mexico because it appeared to be the only authority capable of protecting British commercial interests in an otherwise anarchic situation.[2] His action angered Wilson who was endeavouring to secure a

[1] There is nothing so consistent in the sixty years of Churchill's political life as his championship of Anglo-American understanding, from his lecture tour of 1900 in which he outlined to American audiences the British case in the Boer War, to his efforts on a visit to the United States early in 1959 to assuage any irritation produced by the incorrigible candour of Lord Montgomery. He never underestimated the importance of American public opinion which he cultivated with supreme success. Unapproachable to British reporters, he enjoyed turning American press conferences into historic occasions.

[2] Viscount Grey of Fallodon, *Twenty Five Years, 1892–1916*, Vol. II, pp. 94–5.

better order in Latin America. The President not only himself refused to recognize Huerta, but secured also the withdrawal of British recognition.[1] This affair shows to what end recognition is usually employed by each country. For the Americans it has become a means of putting pressure upon foreign nations: if to have relations with the United States is a privilege, then relations will be permitted only if the United States thinks fit. Thus in 1918, by refusing to deal with the Imperial Government of Germany, Wilson was largely responsible for its overthrow. Non-recognition in peacetime is rarely as effective as this, but the intention is the same. At the time of the Manchurian Crisis in 1932, the American Government tried to discourage aggression by declaring in the Stimson Note that no change so brought about would be recognized. Britain, however, has rarely been able to lay down the law in this way. The least self-sufficient of all the great powers, it is not for her to impose, but to come to terms. She was the first major power to recognize Soviet Russia, and the United States was the last.[2] She was the first non-Communist great power to recognize the People's Republic of China, and, again, the United States looks like being the last. There are, of course, exceptions to this pattern but they have arisen only in abnormal circumstances.[3] In the main, because on the one hand the United States is a large, rich, self-reliant power with idealistic and even revolutionary traditions, and because on the other hand Britain is the world's greatest trading nation, having many scattered interests and responsibilities and an empirical outlook in foreign affairs, the one tends to be much

---

[1] Arthur S. Link, *Woodrow Wilson and the Progressive Era, 1910–17*, pp. 119–20.

[2] Britain recognized the Soviet Union *de facto* in 1921, and *de jure* in 1924. United States recognition was delayed until 1933.

[3] From 1932 Britain for a time took the Stimson line in the League of Nations, but being pledged to a system of collective security, she could hardly in the circumstances have done otherwise. With the breakdown of this system there was a return to normal practice; in an effort to improve relations with Italy, the British Government recognized in 1938 the Italian conquest of Abyssinia. Britain's refusal to recognize Vichy France and the American recognition at Yalta of a Soviet puppet group as the legal government of Poland were wartime contingencies. They show, however, that in the last resort decisions on recognition must conform to immediate political needs.

more discriminating in her recognition of changes than the other.

These differences have come to be reflected in the legal arguments put up by each government to justify its policy. The British position is that provided a government enjoys, with a reasonable prospect of permanency, the obedience of the mass of the population and the effective control of the bulk of the national territory, there is a legal obligation to recognize it.[1] The American view is that recognition is a privilege which no government is entitled to unless it meets the tests of popular support and of willingness and ability to perform its international obligations.[2] Each side has attempted to justify its attitude towards the recognition of Communist China in these terms. Although, judged by the traditional practice of states and by the weight of legal authority, the British case is probably the stronger in law, the question remains one upon which international lawyers are divided. Certainly neither case as it was presented escaped charges of legal inconsistency or faulty reasoning.[3]

That the Americans would probably follow precedent in the case of Communist China was apparent as early as August 1949 when the White Paper on United States relations with China was published. In his covering letter Acheson, the Secretary of State, wrote:

We continue to believe that . . . ultimately the profound civilization and democratic individualism of China will reassert themselves and she will throw off the foreign yoke. I consider that we should encourage all developments in China which now and in the future will work towards this end.

Nothing could be further from the British view than this. In

[1] See Professor Lauterpacht, 'Recognition of Governments', *The Times*, 6 January 1950.

[2] See State Department Memorandum, *State Department Bulletin 1002*, pp. 285–90, 8 September 1958.

[3] For a lawyer's criticism of Lauterpacht's arguments see Dr. G. Schwarzenberger's letter to *The Times*, 9 January 1950. For a criticism of the State Department's arguments, see J. E. S. Fawcett, 'Some Recent Applications of International Law by the United States', *The British Year Book of International Law, 1959*, pp. 246–50. See also: Ti-Chiang Chen, *The International Law of Recognition with Special Reference to Practice in Great Britain and the United States* (1951).

Britain Chinese Communism was regarded as a permanency rooted, if not in the affections, at least in the interests of a peasantry previously exploited and ravaged. Therefore any attempt by the West to interfere in the internal affairs of China would be futile, as well as harmful to Western and especially British interests. Trade would be cut off, assets lost, and the position of Hong Kong perhaps made untenable. The Americans, however, had little interest in trade with China or, at that time, in Hong Kong. They thought the former would only increase Communist war potential,[1] and they were not prepared to help defend the latter.[2] They evacuated the bulk of their officials and businessmen as the Communists advanced. For them the break was complete.

Nevertheless it seems that Bevin was not without hope that American policy might be changed, or at least modified at not too distant a date. Anglo–American exchanges on the course to be adopted had taken place throughout the summer, and in September Bevin and Acheson together discussed the matter.[3] There were later reports that Acheson himself was not so intransigent on recognition as he appeared; the immovable object was the American people.

Many Americans that summer were in a bitter, frustrated and suspicious mood. China had been no ordinary foreign country; she had occupied a unique place in American sentiment. She had been the special field of American missionary endeavour, and there was hardly a Sunday-school in the United States which did not have its China Mission box. Moreover, Americans felt that they and the Chinese had much in common. Both had been the victims of European oppression but had preserved their independence; both had overthrown monarchical government; both had chosen the path of progressive liberalism and democracy. The presence at American universities of numbers of cultivated, softly-spoken, middle-class Chinese students who professed enthusiasm for American ideals and economic and technical achievements, served further to build up this pleasing picture. Thus the sudden transformation of a country that so many had supposed to be liberal,

---

[1] *Daily Telegraph*, Diplomatic Correspondent, 16 September 1949.
[2] *Survey of International Affairs, 1949–50*, p. 335.
[3] Ibid., p. 333.

democratic in intent, tolerant of Christianity and pro-American, into one regarding missionaries as agents of imperialism, philanthropy as economic aggression, and the United States as the arch-enemy, gave the American people an emotional shock from which they have not fully recovered. Not surprisingly a myth arose. The Chinese, it was held, could never willingly have adopted so unnatural a creed as Communism. China had fallen because of Russian aggression on the one side and mismanagement and treachery on the other. The Peking régime was an imposed tyranny; the mass of the Chinese people were still faithful to Chiang Kai-shek. These delusions, although not universal, were actively fostered by the President's Republican opponents, and so became widespread and influential. Indeed, within a year it was becoming 'un-American' to express contrary opinions. In such circumstances, the Administration could not have recognized Communist China without weakening its chances of carrying the mid-term Congressional elections in 1950. Only if Peking had behaved with patience and moderation might a *de facto* recognition eventually have been hazarded. Such, however, was the reverse of Chinese desires or intentions. In Mukden on 24 October 1949 the Communists gaoled the American consul-general and four of his staff after having kept them under house arrest for nearly a year. Similar provocations soon followed, culminating in the seizure of American consular property in Peking. For the time being, recognition by the United States, from being improbable, had become impossible.

At the end of 1949, therefore, the Attlee Government was faced with a perplexing problem. It favoured recognition for a variety of reasons. Being Socialist, it was opposed to the boycotting of Asian national movements which, although supersensitive, xenophobic, and generally awkward, none the less embodied the sentiments and aspirations of the masses. Added to this it was under strong pressure to recognize from all the Far Eastern traders and experts.[1] The object was only partly the safeguarding of commerce and assets. Those who had first-hand experience of China were convinced that the Chinese were far too individualistic to run for long in harness with the Russians.

[1] Bevin. H.C. Debs. Vol. 475. Col. 2082 (24 May 1950). See also Appendix I, The China Association.

From this sprang the idea, taken up in British official circles, that the promotion of trade with China, by making her less dependent upon the Soviet Union, would help to weaken the link between the two.[1] In the Government's view the breaking down of diplomatic isolation was equally important.[2] 'I believe that we were right', said Bevin later, 'to recognize the People's Government and not leave the Russians to assume that . . . they were the only country to do anything at all for China.'[3] Apart, however, from these broader aims, China touched Britain too closely for relations to lapse without the possibility of grave repercussions. The vulnerability and economic dependence upon the mainland of Hong Kong had to be considered. So, too, had the interests and nationalistic sentiments of the five millions of Chinese domiciled on British territory.[4]

But the arguments against recognition were equally cogent. The step would mean a rift between the policies of the two leading Western powers, and this the Communists must be expected to exploit to the full. It would also damage the reputation of Britain with the American public at a time when, owing to their prevailing mood, their influence could be potent. It would cause a split in the Commonwealth, for while the United States refused to recognize so would Canada, Australia and New Zealand, who all depended for their defence upon the American mastery of the Pacific.[5] Neither South Africa, inherently anti-Communist, nor France, fighting a desperate battle in Indo-China, could be expected to follow the British lead. And apart from these external divisions, there would also be trouble at home. Recognition without the United States would be opposed by most Conservatives. Although the Government enjoyed a large majority and could override the Opposition, party controversy in foreign affairs, avoided since the war, was not good.

As Bevin admitted later, the decision was a difficult one to make.[6] At first it seemed that the Government did not wish to

---

[1] *Daily Telegraph*, Diplomatic Correspondent, 16 September 1949.
[2] K. Younger (Minister of State). H.C. Debs. Vol. 475. Cols. 2186–7 (24 May 1950).   [3] Bevin. Ibid. Col. 2083.
[4] Lord Jowitt. H.L. Debs. Vol. 166. Col. 89 (7 March 1950).
[5] Although there was some reluctance in New Zealand to act differently from Britain.   [6] H.C. Debs. Vol. 475. Col. 2082 (24 May 1950).

act out of step with the United States. On 25 October, Dr. Evatt, the Australian Minister for External Affairs, stated that London, Washington, and Canberra were agreed that before recognition could be granted Chinese assurances would be required respecting the integrity of neighbouring countries, including Hong Kong, and the keeping of international obligations.[1] Even as late as 14 December, the Under Secretary reaffirmed that no decision had been reached and that the Government was still in consultation with and wished to act with others.[2] Yet on 6 January 1950, without asking for any guarantees or assurances, and without securing simultaneous action by her great ally or her oldest and closest Dominions, Britain proceeded to recognize *de jure* the People's Republic of China.

From the Foreign Secretary's explanation later in the year it is apparent that the deciding factor was the attitude of the Asian members of the Commonwealth.[3] On 30 December India recognized Communist China, and within a week so had Pakistan and Ceylon. The Colombo Conference, which would help to determine future relations between Britain and these countries, was about to be held. Moreover, the Labour Government attached great importance to Asian public opinion, and to that of India in particular. The friendship, or at least benevolent neutrality of this vast and influential nation had been a prime object of British policy since the granting of independence in 1947—and indeed had led to that decision. But success in this appeared to depend to a more than usual degree upon the exercise of patience and discretion. All the newly independent Asian states were extremely touchy. They feared a return of Western influence or control exercised more subtly than in the past, and they wished to banish, as far as possible, the reminders of their late subjection. With new Asia in this state of mind, the question of Chinese recognition took on wider implications. The Indians especially, saw in China's latest revolution the counterpart of their own successful struggle for independence and status. For them, that it was Asian meant everything, that it was Communist was almost irrelevant. If, therefore, none of the Western powers recognized Communist China, this might

---

[1] *The Times*, 26 October 1949.
[2] C. Mayhew, H.C. Debs. Vol. 470. Col. 257.
[3] Bevin. Ibid. Vol. 475. Cols. 2081–4 (24 May 1950).

be taken as a rebuff to Asian nationalism, as evidence that the
Commonwealth's claim to be an inter-racial community was
an idle boast, and that in the last resort the loyalty of the white
members would always be to their own kind. Suspicions on this
point were easily aroused; many Asians believed that the atomic
bomb would never have been used against the Germans. Presuming such an assessment to be correct, much would depend
on the British attitude, for in India, Pakistan, and Ceylon,
Britain was more readily identified with the white West than
any other power. If she had to part company with the United
States and the older Dominions, the bonds with these were, in
contrast, strong and tried.

The Government recognized Communist China while Parliament was in recess, so that immediate reactions are difficult to
estimate. Most of the leading newspapers responded favourably
however. *The Times*, *Manchester Guardian*, *Observer* and *Spectator*,
although regretting that the policies of Britain and the United
States had diverged, set out the reasons for the Government's
action and considered the decision a wise one despite the attitude of the United States. *The Times*, with its tendency to speak
as though from a little behind and a little above the right
shoulder of a Left-wing government (or the left shoulder of a
Right) was noticeably unconstrained. On 2 January it had
criticized in detail American policy over China and remarked
that the first essential was to realize that what had happened
would not soon be changed—'the tide cannot be kept out with
a broom'; on 7 January it added that Anglo-American friendship 'would not be well served by meekly deferring to the judgement of the United States. . . .' *The Economist*, however, was not
happy. Having, as became its business interests and geography
of circulation, an essentially trans-Atlantic outlook, it spoke of
any possible gain from recognition as derisory when compared
with the harm done to Anglo-American relations. The *Daily
Telegraph* too, in a foretaste of what was to come from a greatly
augmented Opposition, described the step as a 'hasty and ill-
considered decision after months of hesitation and drift'.

Parliament reassembled early in March after a general
election in which the Government had retained power by a
majority of only six. By this time it was clear that recognition,
by not leading to full diplomatic relations, had achieved far

less than had been hoped, and indeed had landed Britain in an embarrassing situation. The Opposition, intent on getting the Government out, were in no mood to give any quarter. In both Houses recognition was attacked on nearly every ground. To Lord Salisbury, a leading critic, it was 'a blunder of the first water', an act of panic; Lord Mancroft held that it would encourage the Malayan bandits; Lord Killearn stated that the prospect of Chinese Communist consuls in Malaya filled people with alarm; Sir Patrick Spens believed that no one else had been consulted; almost all regarded it as having been premature and deplored its effect upon the United States, Canada, Australia and New Zealand.[1]

The Tory onslaught might have been modified by the very argument which tipped the balance—the need to conciliate Asian and especially Indian opinion. But it was not. In the course of a debate on 24 May, Eden spoke of the opportunities given to Peking to play off Britain against the United States.[2] This became a commonplace, but that there were much better opportunities of exploiting differences between London and New Delhi was either conveniently forgotten, never considered, or dismissed as of only secondary importance. Earlier Captain Gammans had asked whether Britain was under any obligation to India.[3]

In truth, Asian opinion never had the significance for the Right that it had for the Left. R. B. McCallum has described Tories as 'power-snobs'[4] and certainly, compared with the United States, new Asia was militarily negligible. But this is probably only a partial explanation of the Tory attitude. These new states possessed a character, and their governments an outlook, bound to make a very one-sided impact upon British political sentiment. For Tories it was distressing to contemplate the dissolution of the proud empires which only ten years before had exerted in these areas a glittering, profitable and seemingly permanent sway. But to make matters worse the viceroys and

[1] H.L. Debs. Vol. 166. Cols. 41–2 (7 March 1950); Col. 748 (4 April 1950); Col. 875 (5 April 1950); H.C. Debs. Vol. 473. Cols. 1381–2 (6 April 1950).

[2] H.C. Debs. Vol. 475. Cols. 2071–2.

[3] Ibid. Vol. 472. Col. 225 (7 March 1950).

[4] *Public Opinion and the Last Peace*, pp. 120, 122.

D

governors had been replaced by all manner of political and religious cranks. India was not the most peculiar in this respect; its independence day had not been postponed by astrologers as had the Burmese, nor was it in danger of becoming a theocracy. In fact, by Western standards, India was the most orthodoxly governed of them all. But it was also the largest, and its policies were irritating. To many Tories it must have appeared uncommonly like the London School of Economics erected into a system of government.[1] Nehru was frequently attacked by the Tory press, expecially the *Daily Express*, for his indulgent attitude towards Communism and his habit of sermonizing upon the sins of colonialism. Moreover, having declared itself unwilling to remain under the Crown, the Indian Government proclaimed the country a republic in January 1950. This seemed a more radical step at the time than it does in retrospect. It would not be surprising if during the recognition controversy the majority of Tories were of the opinion that if the Indians were bent on going the way of the Irish, it was hardly worth trying to stop them.

What verdict should be passed upon the British Government's recognition of Communist China early in 1950, and upon the arguments used in its favour? If we consider what was hoped for and what was obtained, then unquestionably recognition was a sorry failure. When granted *de jure*, it is normally followed by the exchange of ambassadors. But to this Peking would not agree. It merely accepted a *chargé d'affaires* and then, when not keeping him waiting for long periods, suffered him to see but minor officials. In explanation of this conduct the Communists quoted the British plea—intended for American rather than Chinese consumption—that recognition did not mean approval. They also referred to the detention in Hong Kong (pending the outcome of legal proceedings) of certain aircraft they claimed, and to the British decision to abstain rather than vote in favour of Peking's representation at the United Nations.

---

[1] It should scarcely be necessary to point out that by 1950 L.S.E. was no longer the citadel of socialist-pacifist-intellectualism that it may have been in the 1930s, although this reputation still lingered. Nevertheless, like the *New Statesman*, the School of the Laski era appears to have had a decisive impact upon the Indian intelligentsia. See: N. C. Chaudhuri, *A Passage to England*, p. 156.

This indeed showed that to approach a Communist power with no card to play, merely trusting to a favourable response, was to put oneself in a false position. But it showed more. The intimation that Britain must first undergo a change of heart, and the treatment accorded the British Government's representative, were redolent not so much of Communist intransigence— even at the height of the Cold War Soviet diplomacy was noted for its correctness—as of the contemptuously condescending reception of George III's emissary by the Son of Heaven in 1816. This display of traditional Chinese arrogance boded ill for the future.

There could now be little prospect of China's being won away from Russia, at least in the short run. In fact the ties were strengthened. On 14 February, a little more than a month after British recognition, a Sino–Soviet Treaty of Friendship, Alliance and Mutual Assistance was signed. This was followed on 19 April by a general trade agreement. Although British trade was kept going in a limited way, it was soon found increasingly difficult for firms to continue operating in China itself. Oppressed by ruinous official interference, British businessmen eventually cut their losses and left the country. Within two and a half years the vast British assets remaining in China had been lost.[1]

Thus, in some respects at least, were the critics proved right. But what was the alternative? Some favoured *de facto* rather than *de jure* recognition, or a postponement until the time was more propitious. *De facto* recognition, however, would have been worse than useless. It is usually granted to a régime whose stability is doubtful and it does not involve the formal exchange of diplomatic representatives. Hence it would have had some of the unfortunate repercussions of *de jure* recognition but none of its looked-for benefits. In any case the Chinese made it plain that they wanted *de jure* recognition or nothing.[2] As for a postponement until such time as the Chinese should show themselves willing to engage in friendly relations, there was no

---

[1] The usual Chinese method was to encourage the laying of claims against a firm (particularly by employees) until they equalled its assets. Then, after the signing of an agreement by which the Chinese Government took over the firm's debts, the British staff were permitted to leave the country.

[2] G. L. Goodwin, *Britain and the United Nations*, p. 119.

evidence that they ever would. Indeed, the political climate in the Far East might, as in fact it did, get much worse, and there were valuable assets at stake. This was the Chinese trump card. It must have been abundantly clear to them that the British need for diplomatic relations was much greater than their own, and so Peking determined to make the most of its chance.

But in dealing with the question of timing, we must remember that the British Government felt it necessary to fall into line with India, Pakistan, and Ceylon. Did it over-emphasize this aspect of the matter? The question is not easy to answer, but it is doubtful whether the British decision had much effect on Asian public opinion or whether not to have acted at once would have led to serious consequences. Suez was much more of a shock to Asian sensibilities, yet India, Pakistan, and Ceylon remained in the Commonwealth. Moreover, although the importance of presenting a common Anglo–Asian front is not to be denied, the outcome in this case was unfortunate. For by welcoming the Asian approach (an Indian ambassador was at once accepted) but snubbing the British, the Chinese could exploit those jealousies and differences that British policy had been designed to overcome.

If Britain's action was only doubtfully advantageous in the East, in the West it brought its crop of problems. British and American policies were now set on different courses and collisions were inevitable. Throughout 1950 Britain tried to get Communist China seated at the United Nations, but was thwarted in her efforts by the United States. Similarly in 1951 the British Government endeavoured to ensure that Peking and not Nationalist China was a signatory to the Japanese Peace Treaty, but again, after the matter had been left to the free choice of Japan, American pressure was applied and the treaty was concluded with the Nationalists. This caused some ill-feeling at the time.[1]

Did recognition, then, do any good? One fortunate result was that Britain's having some sort of relationship with Peking naturally placed Eden in a better position for mediating in the negotiations which brought peace to Indo-China in 1954. As a general consideration, however, there is always something to be gained by making the first move even if one suffers a rebuff.

[1] See below, p. 138.

At least one does not become a prey to doubts, regrets and self-recrimination afterwards. As it happened, the British were tolerably well united over the Korean War. But is it not conceivable that without recognition and the subsequent snub, without the attempts afterwards made by the British Government to get Communist China into the United Nations, British radical opinion, still to some extent embodying the conscience of the West, would have regarded the war with very different feelings?

Thus recognition involved a risk, and although there were some later and incidental advantages, the direct results had proved unfortunate. But should policies or actions be judged solely by their results? It is said that Venizelos, on reading in Fisher's *History of Europe* that his Smyrna campaign was a mistake, ironically observed that every policy which did not succeed was a mistake. For if statesmen did not occasionally take risks, would they achieve anything? Indeed, a statesman may sometimes be well-advised to take a considerable risk if the prize is proportionately great—in other words, a wise man will sometimes back an outsider. The argument may be taken too far. If the stake is everything—as it was for Austria in July 1914—it will be foolish to gamble. The risk must first be calculated in terms of probable losses against possible gains. Judged in these terms, and remembering that the Anglo–American connexion is the strongest and soundest in the world, the British recognition of Communist China does not appear to have been such a blunder.

Moreover, the only real alternative was non-recognition, and it may be seriously questioned whether this is not a dangerous anachronism in the present age, at least as far as the great powers are concerned. For not only is it, as a means of exerting pressure, entirely inadequate when applied to a large, self-contained and efficient totalitarian state, but it leaves unresolved a situation which is certain to be exploited by all whose interest it is to upset the *status quo*. Moreover, the absence of diplomatic contact between two or more of the great powers is certainly unsatisfactory and may be dangerous. This was frequently stressed by British spokesmen in the United Nations. It was also the argument which Churchill used when claiming that there was a good *prima facie* case for the recognition of Peking.

If diplomacy cannot always smooth, it may at least be able to clarify relations between states. However bad relations may be, it is better that each side should become familiar with the outlook, intentions, and aspirations of the other, than to grope and blunder in ignorance, a prey to rumour and self-delusion. Of course, the force of this argument is greatly lessened at a time of severe ideological conflict when mutual suspicion may prove insuperable or when one side is bent upon the destruction of the other. Japanese diplomacy, it may be recalled, was engaged in lulling the United States into a sense of false security on the eve of Pearl Harbour. Yet where there is a common interest— coexistence or even a restriction of conflict—the need for one side to be able to reach the other without resorting to third parties or to declarations which might be mistaken for propaganda, becomes evident. Such arguments undoubtedly influenced opinion during the 1950s, when few in Britain attacked the recognition of Communist China and almost all wished for a change in the American attitude.

III

The Chinese Seat

The next problem raised by the establishment of Communist China was that of Chinese representation at the United Nations. China was an original member of the Organization and had a permanent seat on the Security Council. It followed that her legal government had the right to represent her. But whether this government was at Peking or in Formosa was naturally a matter of dispute amongst United Nations members. Since by the beginning of 1950 only a small minority of countries had recognized the Communist régime, the Kuomintang delegation continued to speak, vote and act in the name of China. Whether this situation should continue or Peking be allowed to occupy the Chinese seat was strongly debated in the Western world, for it touched important issues. In Britain three aspects of the question particularly engaged attention: the effect upon Western and British interests; the role of the United Nations in a world for which it was not designed; and the cause of peace.

As with recognition, the affair of the Chinese seat again raised the question of the extent to which it was necessary, in view of the uncompromising attitude of the United States towards Peking, to placate Asian nationalism, or at least deprive it of a grievance. Radical opinion habitually stressed the rise of Asia as an inevitable and irresistible process which it was wise to concur with, and foolish, as well as immoral, to oppose. This view certainly influenced the policies of the Labour Government, as shown in the preceding chapter. But it was also one which could not consistently be translated into political action. Not every change could be reconciled with British interests, and although a certain strain might safely be put upon the Anglo–American connexion when times were tranquil, in moments of crisis it was important to remember that British security depended ultimately upon American power.

In consequence, British policy on the question of the Chinese seat was several times modified or changed. When, at the beginning of 1950, the Russians first proposed that a Chinese Communist delegation should be admitted and the Nationalists expelled, the majority of Security Council members, including the United States, voted against. Britain abstained, the proposal being regarded as 'premature'.[1] Yet within two months Bevin was making every effort to get Peking seated, and the reason for this, at least in part, seems once more to have been concern about the effect upon Asian opinion.

On 13 January, the Russians, unable to get their way, abruptly left the Security Council and did not return. Over the next few months this performance was repeated in all the other United Nations bodies in which the voting on the Chinese seat went against them. Bevin first saw the boycott as an attempt to bully the Council into giving way. The Government, he declared later, had refused to be hurried, especially as full diplomatic relations had yet to be accepted by Peking.[2] Yet when in mid-March he began to canvass members of the Security Council in support of Peking's admission, he did so without even making sure that Britain, or the West generally, would derive some compensating benefit. It is likely that the Government regarded the matter as one of principle which should not be made the subject of bargaining, but Britain was under no obligation to take the initiative, and so long as Peking refused to receive a British ambassador, had every excuse for not doing so. Apart from the general radical conviction that the entry of Communist China into the community of nations was wise, lawful, and proper, there were two immediate motives. One was a desire to see the United Nations, unsettled by the Soviet boycott, functioning again.[3] The other is suggested by an observation which Bevin made later in the year:

. . . although it may seem strange, I never believed that Russia wanted China in the United Nations. I think Russia kept putting her up in the belief that the Western nations would turn down the idea, so that Russia could use that fact to make enemies for Western nations. I never believed that the walking-out business was anything more than a set of stage supers playing a very poor part.[4]

---

[1] Security Council, *Official Records, 1950*, No. 1, p. 6, 459th Meeting (10 January 1950).

[2] H.C. Debts. Vol. 475. Col. 2084 (24 May 1950).

[3] Ibid. Cols. 2085–6.   [4] Ibid. Vol. 482. Col. 1458 (14 December 1950).

Here Bevin seems to have glimpsed the truth: that the Communists were chiefly interested in the United Nations as a means of influencing opinion in the uncommitted countries. If a policy of bluster and ostentatious withdrawal was designed to keep the issue alive, to convince Asians that only the Soviet Union sympathized with their aspirations and was prepared to champion their rights, and to have a stiffening effect upon the West the reverse of that ostensibly intended, then the best reply to such tactics was to admit Peking to the United Nations with the least delay.[1]

Bevin's efforts to recruit the seven needed votes in the Security Council were, however, unavailing. France was smarting under Soviet recognition of the rebel Vietminh government, and the United States, although she promised not to veto the motion if it were carried, refused any positive help. Apart from Norway, none of the other members of the Council who had not originally voted in favour of Peking could be won over. Nevertheless the British Government was resolved to press the matter. On 19 June a report from Lake Success stated that Britain would probably no longer abstain but would vote for the admission of Communist China not only in the Security Council, but in other United Nations bodies as well.[2] The direct assault having failed, infiltration was to be tried. But before this could be done war broke out in Korea.

The shock of the North Korean invasion on 25 June 1950 induced the British Government to do nothing further until the situation had become clearer. Too many questions remained unanswered, and for the moment it was natural for the West to close its ranks. The crisis, however, had the effect of focusing far more public attention upon the problem, and, once the initial surprise and apprehension had passed, of strengthening the demand, especially amongst radicals, for the rapid settlement of the question in Peking's favour.

Some, perhaps most, of the advocates of this course were convinced that the adoption of a friendly attitude towards

---

[1] An Indian student of international affairs informed the writer *circa* 1956 that the exclusion of Communist China from the United Nations had done more to damage the reputation of the West in India than anything else.

[2] *The Times*, 20 June 1950. United Nations correspondent.

China was, apart from any idealistic consideration, the policy most likely to serve the national interest. The North Korean aggression was something of an enigma, but it was widely believed to have been instigated by Moscow. How far China was implicated no one knew, but radical opinion had never inclined to the view that Communist China was a satellite of the Soviet Union. If we handle China well, remarked Lord Chorley in July, she might go the way of Yugoslavia. This was an old idea which recent events had done little to substantiate, but many, and not only radicals, considered that a tolerant Western policy would ease tension and perhaps overcome suspicion, whereas an uncompromising one would force Peking into dependence upon Russia and possibly into the war.[1]

The presumption behind this argument, and it coloured radical thinking throughout the Far Eastern crisis, was that the Chinese leaders, if not the creatures of Moscow, must *ipso facto* be rational and reasonable men. That Communist China might be infused with a greater degree of revolutionary fervour and doctrinaire fanaticism than even the Soviet Union, was suspected by few at the time. True, the Yangtse incident and the response to the British recognition had indicated that Peking could be uncompromising and difficult, but such conduct was easily excused: the passage of British warships on the Yangtse was as provoking as would be the presence of Chinese warships on the Thames; and Peking's refusal to have full diplomatic relations was perfectly understandable when it was remembered how close London was to Washington, and Washington to Chiang Kai-shek.[2] Even their invasion of Tibet in October, and their massive intervention in Korea during November 1950, did not entirely dispel the idea that the Chinese Communists were more sinned against than sinning. One body of opinion suggested that but for Peking's exclusion from the United Nations these developments might never have occurred, and that until she was given her rightful place in the counsels of the

---

[1] See: Lord Chorley (Labour), H.L. Debs. Vol. 168. Col. 793 (26 July 1950); *The Times*, leader, 7 August 1950; *New Statesman*, 2 September 1950; *Spectator*, 13 October and 24 November 1950; T. E. N. Driberg (Labour), H.C. Debs. Vol. 481. Col. 1385 (30 November 1950).

[2] See, for example, letter from F. A. B. Jones, *Sunday Times*, 31 December 1950.

nations, there was small likelihood that peace would return to the Far East.[1]

This conclusion needs to be looked at more closely. It implied that if Communist delegates were admitted, an intolerable provocation would be ended, and, through diplomatic intercourse, suspicion and apprehension would be dispelled and common problems eventually resolved. It implied also that the continued presence of the Kuomintang at the United Nations constituted a threat to the security of China which Peking would be impelled to counter. Undoubtedly the position of Nationalist China as one of the Big Five at the Security Council was absurd, and to the bulk of Asian opinion, exasperating, but to suggest that this was largely responsible for China's resorting to force indicates an ignorance of Communist theory and practice.

To a Communist régime, every non-Communist power is a potential enemy. The threat to Peking did not lie in Chiang's being represented at the United Nations—whether he was or not made little difference—but in the backing of the Nationalists by American power. Further, it is not necessary to explain Chinese policy simply in terms of self-defence. The Korean intervention was in part defensive, but unless the term is stretched to cover almost any military or political move, of neither Indo-China nor Tibet could the same be said. China's behaviour throughout the 1950s, culminating in the unprovoked invasion of India's Himalayan borderlands in 1959, demonstrated that Peking, like most régimes impelled by a revolutionary ideology, was prepared to probe and push until stopped.

Admittedly these tendencies were less apparent in 1950, but why were they not expected, or why, from such indications as had appeared, were not the right conclusions drawn? The answer seems to lie in a general reluctance to believe that Peking was an orthodox Communist régime, or to accept the implications if she was. We have already examined the first of

---

[1] See: Lord Perth (Deputy Liberal Leader in the House of Lords and formerly, as Sir Eric Drummond, the first Secretary General of the League of Nations), H.L. Debs. Vol. 169. Col. 289 (15 November 1950); Lord Samuel (Liberal Leader in the House of Lords), Ibid. Col. 999 (14 December 1950); Lord Stansgate (Labour), Ibid. Col. 1039.

these; the second arises out of an unwillingness to accept the idea of the inevitability of conflict. This, which is fundamental to Marxist–Leninism, many liberal-minded people, and perhaps English people in particular, find it difficult to take seriously. They dismiss it as a myth invented by militarists or as an ephemeral revolutionary slogan. Moreover, brought up in an integrated and well-ordered society, and succeeding to a philosophical heritage embracing such classical rationalist assumptions as the world community and the harmony of interests, they tend to view, and treat, irreconcilable conflicts as though they were simply cases of misunderstanding. Hence the bringing of the disputants together is looked upon as being half-way to a settlement. If only each side could learn the other's point of view, could discover that its own fears were groundless, its opponent's understandable, what need then for a conflict which at heart none desired?

This type of argument played its part in the case put up for the admission of the Chinese Communists to the United Nations. If, it was claimed, they could be reassured that the Western allies were not out to encompass their destruction, there was surely no reason why a great and ruinous war should be fought over Korea and Formosa. Such a view was, of course, unrealistic because it naïvely ignored the dynamism of revolution on the one hand, and the state of the American mind—and of the American military mind in particular—on the other. Equally unreal, however, was the assumption that the United Nations was a necessary medium for serious diplomatic intercourse.

Here was another relic of Wilsonian liberalism in international affairs—the belief that all diplomacy should be open and, so far as peace and security were concerned, centred upon the world institution. In fact, open diplomacy usually degenerates into 'playing to the gallery', and diplomacy that means business is best conducted in a different environment. When two or more powers wish to engage in serious diplomatic discussions with a view to getting results, they prefer to make their own arrangements and to deal with each other directly. In this respect it was unfortunate that the United States had not recognized Peking. But even so, Peking was not cut off from the West except by her own choice. To say that her absence from the United Nations was an insuperable obstacle to peace was absurd. Had she any real desire to make contact, she could have restored ambassadorial relations with an only too willing Britain, or negotiated through India or some other intermediary. In truth, the United States and Communist China were in a state of uncompromising enmity. Whatever might be said in favour of Peking's admission to the United Nations, the confrontation there of two such opponents, far from improving the atmosphere, would simply have given their contention a greater publicity.

Nevertheless, there was a possible advantage to be gained from letting this occur. Despite the stream of anti-Western and particularly anti-American propaganda emanating from Peking, the West remained in much uncertainty during the early months of the Korean War as to what Communist China was likely to do or was prepared to do in a swiftly changing situation. The presence of her representatives at the United Nations might have done something both to shed light on this and to reveal any divergence that might have existed between the views of Peking and Moscow. This point was not lost upon the British Government. The Government was under no illusion, said Lord Addison in July, that in the Security Council the Western powers would probably be faced with a new opponent and a second veto, but at least they would know where they stood.[1] Indeed, two experienced British diplomats, Sir Gladwyn Jebb and Gerald Fitzmaurice, were later to contend that had Peking been represented at the United Nations at the time, the North Korean invasion, or at any rate China's intervention, might never have occurred.[2] This was not a repetition of the liberal argument that there would then have been no cause for conflict, but that each side, by being better acquainted with the other's position and intentions, would have acted less rashly. Even Lord Salisbury, a persistent opponent of recognition and of Peking's being given the seat, welcomed the invitation accorded to the Chinese Communists in November to send a representative to the Security Council to discuss the grave situation in Korea.[3] The result of this invitation—a refusal to

[1] H.L. Debs. Vol. 168. Cols. 889–90 (26 July 1950).
[2] See G. L. Goodwin, *Britain and the United Nations*, p. 125.
[3] H.L. Debs. Vol. 169. Cols. 279–80 (15 November 1950).

discuss Korea but a vitriolic attack upon the United States and her Formosa policy[1]—certainly exposed the vanity of any hopes that Peking's membership of the United Nations would lead to fruitful negotiations, but at least it did something to dispel such doubts as still existed about the Chinese Communist attitude. Membership might indeed have provided a more detailed revelation.

Until now we have examined the case for Peking's admission so far as it concerned Western interests and the cause of peace. There was, however, a further side to the question: its bearing upon the future of the United Nations as a world institution.

The United Nations Organization had grown out of the war-time Grand Alliance, the idea being that if they remained as united after as they had been during the war, the great powers could effectively ensure world peace and stability. The instrument for achieving these ends was the Security Council, upon which the Big Five (China, France, the Soviet Union, the United Kingdom and the United States) were permanently represented. In effect the nations had intended to set up a Hobbesian sovereign whose authority in all matters touching upon peace and security would be supreme. Unfortunately there could be no more unpromising foundation for a Hobbesian world order than the transient wartime alliance between Western democracy and Russian Communism. With the elimination of the Fascist threat there was nothing to hold such divergent and antagonistic systems together. Although some useful work was done in the economic and social fields, the cold war made nonsense of the United Nations as a means of preserving world order. The members of the all-powerful Security Council disagreed on almost every issue; the Hobbesian sovereign had turned out to be little better than King Log.

Not everyone, however, was discouraged by this. One body of opinion, largely but not exclusively radical, instead of condemning or dismissing it for its ineffectiveness, rejoiced that the Organization embraced both sides in the great conflict which

[1] The Security Council invited Peking to send a representative on two occasions: on 29 September 1950 to discuss Formosa, and on 8 November to answer charges of intervention in Korea. The second invitation was rejected, the first accepted in November. The Americans had wanted a summons, not an invitation.

dominated the post-war scene. Its near universality—something never approached by the League of Nations—they regarded as a priceless asset, and saw in it the hope of ultimate world unity. These opinions were partly a legacy from the League of Nations era, for although the League was dead, many radicals of the older generation had never lost faith in its principles. It was not, they maintained, the League that had failed; cynical and short-sighted politicians had failed the League. Hence some of the notions which had been current in the 1920s were applied to the new institution. Even members of the Labour Government, despite the course events had taken since 1935, were still susceptible to Wilsonian idealism. This was particularly true of Noel-Baker, the Minister of State, who in 1946 declared that Britain would use the United Nations 'to kill power politics'.[1] Bevin, too, at one time shared Noel-Baker's hope that the Organization would be the first step on the road to world government.[2]

The fullest expression of this radical internationalism was to be found in the view that the United Nations should be a 'Parliament of Man'. Appropriately its chief exponent was one of the last survivors of Asquith's government. In a speech to the House of Lords on 26 July 1950, Lord Samuel expressed a hope dating from the hey-day of English liberalism:

We cannot [he said] yet secure in this age Tennyson's Federation of the World, but we might secure the Parliament of Man.[3]

Again, later in the year, he declared:

The question is, in fact, is the United Nations to be an alliance of anti-Communist states, or is it to be a Parliament of Man? That is the vital question. . . . It is of vital importance that all should be

[1] H.C. Debs. Vol. 419. Col. 1262 (20 February 1946). Noel-Baker was awarded the Nobel Peace Prize in 1959.

[2] Bevin, Ibid. Vol. 416. Cols. 785–6 (23 November 1945); Noel-Baker, Ibid. Vol. 418. Cols. 630–1 (28 January 1946). See G. L. Goodwin, *Britain and the United Nations*, p. 52.

[3] H.L. Debs. Vol. 168. Col. 750. A reference to *Locksley Hall*, published in 1842. The lines:

'Till the war-drum throbb'd no longer, and the battle flags were furl'd
 In the Parliament of Man, the Federation of the World.'
largely made Tennyson's reputation as a poet of unexampled progress. Ironically they follow a prediction of aerial warfare.

got together for discussion in one room and round one table, in the full blaze of world publicity; and that they should there defend their causes at the table in a single organization responsible to mankind as a whole. That, and that alone, is the general principle to be applied.[1]

This recalls the belief of the League's founders that world opinion, when fully alive to the issues of a dispute, would provide a moral sanction which no government would dare to disregard. The whole conception was a fallacy, as the events of the 1930s soon proved. For not only does it underestimate the power of governments—particularly their great, and in some cases, absolute influence over opinion—but it presupposes the recognition and acceptance of common standards. In the early 1920s, when the League was dominated by the democracies and when world public opinion was little more than a synonym for Anglo-Saxon public opinion, the idea was not altogether an unreasonable one. But in the world as left by the Second World War, in large part tyrannically governed, ideologically riven, and inflamed with nationalism, any idea that world public opinion could be appealed to like a jury, and, like a jury, come to unanimous, independent and compulsive decisions was manifestly absurd. True, a fancied revival of old-fashioned imperialism may be relied upon to raise a near universal outcry, but that is the exception which proves the rule.

In the main, however, the case for the universality of the United Nations, and hence the admission of Communist China, was only incidentally concerned with the possible mobilization of world opinion. In 1950, the United Nations as it was then constituted seemed to many to fulfil a more urgent and a more fundamental need. The cold war had severed almost every link between the Communist *bloc* and the West. Except for diplomatic personnel, practically no one was allowed to pass from one to the other. Liaison in occupied Germany had ceased, or was reduced to a sterile formality. Soviet wives had been prevented from joining their British or American husbands. Cultural and sporting exchanges had lapsed. No Russian athletes had attended the 1948 Olympic Games. Economically each side was self-sufficient. Against this dismal background, the United Nations alone seemed to symbolize that the world was still one.

[1] H.L. Debs. Vol. 169. Col. 1002 (14 December 1950).

That the debates there were often mere slanging matches was even taken as an encouraging sign. 'Better jaw, jaw, than war, war', remarked Churchill, and the sentiment was frequently expressed. Yet there was a more positive side to the universalist case than a wry belief in the comradeship of invective. It was assumed, for one thing, that the very business of being and working together would gradually instil a sense of toleration, which, whether it percolated back to governments or not, was worth fostering. Partly this was a reflection of British Parliamentary experience. In answer to a suggestion that the Chinese Communists, if admitted, would simply cause extra trouble, Bevin replied that this would be of little consequence, for he was glad to observe that the General Assembly was rapidly developing a temper very much like that of the House of Commons.[1] A Labour peer, Lord Chorley, claimed that apart from being 'good for the United States', the admission of Communist China to the Security Council would enable that body to function better, much of the friction and trouble being caused by Russia's having to play a lone hand.[2] One is reminded of the comment usually made after a general election by supporters of a party returned with a large majority; if only the majority had been a little smaller, they say, how much more alert and vigorous would be the Government, how much more responsible the Opposition.

The danger of this type of thinking is that the political significance of the United Nations can all too easily be exaggerated. Executive power in Britain is concentrated in the House of Commons, so that what the House decides is always important. But the world's power still resides in the world's capitals. A harmonious world institution is no guarantee of a harmonious world, and even heads of government who win success and acclaim internationally may well experience, as did President Wilson and General Smuts, a less welcome outcome domestically. It seems to be characteristic of liberals and radicals that politically they are prone to exercise their talents and spend their energies not where power is, but where they hope it is or think it ought to be.

On the other hand realism, unless tempered with a degree of

[1] H.C. Debs. Vol. 482. Cols. 1457–8 (14 December 1950).
[2] H.L. Debs. Vol. 168. Col. 793 (26 July 1950).

idealism, and in particular a belief in an ultimate harmony of interests, may lead to Nemesis. This came increasingly to be realized after 1949 when the Soviet Union exploded her first atomic bomb, and when it was revealed that bombs of vastly greater power were capable of development. Now that the American monopoly of nuclear weapons was at an end, the case for maintaining every possible contact between East and West seemed to many to be unanswerable. The Security Council had failed to work because the defeat of Fascism had removed a common fear great enough to overshadow the mutual jealousies, suspicions and antagonisms of the major powers. After 1945 they had nothing to fear but each other, so that short of an invasion from outer space it was difficult to imagine that the Security Council, functioning as its founders intended, could ever answer a need. Soviet possession of the atomic bomb, however, transformed the situation. For war itself, if waged without restraint, had now become, or was well on the way to becoming, an overwhelming common danger. Thus, although the peace and security arrangements had proved almost wholly incongruous and irrelevant in a cold war setting, circumstances might now arise so pregnant with danger for all concerned, that states would be glad to avail themselves of the facilities for negotiating which the Organization provided. At least there was much to be said for keeping the universal structure of the United Nations in being.

Such were the practical arguments employed in favour of admitting Communist China to the United Nations. During the opening phase of the Korean War they were resisted on two main counts. The first was that British policy should not depart from American, at any rate not to the extent of sponsoring that which the United States was determined to resist. This we have already examined in connexion with recognition. The second was that the Organization should have as its prime function not the bringing together of East and West, but the taking of effective action against an aggressor.

When North Korean forces began their invasion of the South, the Security Council was able for the first time to take prompt and effective action. This was made possible, however, only by taking advantage of the fortuitous absence of the Russian delegation—still boycotting the proceedings over the

issue of the Chinese seat—and the enforced absence of a Chinese
Communist delegation. If, therefore, the Security Council was
to retain its effectiveness, it followed that this situation would
have to continue. The leading proponent of the view that it
should was Lord Vansittart, a former permanent head of the
Foreign Office who was well-known for his unrelenting hostility to totalitarian government in any form. On 26 July he
wrote to the *Manchester Guardian* with characteristic pungency:

I refer to the notion that all might now be well if only Communist
China were admitted to the Security Council. Exactly why? We
have just got out of the almost moribund United Nations a sign of
life almost entirely due to the United States, simply because the
Kremlinites were absent sulking. It is now suggested that we might
live happy ever after . . . if we could get back the Soviets and their
veto reinforced by that of Soviet China. Again why?[1]

About this, two observations may be made. First, although it
was possible to keep the Chinese Communists out of the
Security Council, the Russians were free to return and exercise
the veto whenever they chose. Secondly, the absence of the
Communist veto did not merely mean the removal of a tire-
some restraint, it posed a fundamental problem: was the United
Nations to be employed as an anti-Communist alliance, prepared if need be to fight two out of five of the world's great
powers? Of course, it could be argued that had the situation
been reversed the Communists would only too eagerly have
seized the chance of arrogating to their cause the name and
prestige of the world institution. Yet not only would the prosecu-
tion of armed conflict by the Security Council against certain of
its permanent members be a travesty of the Council's function,
but it would also result in world war, a recurrence of which the
Organization was chiefly designed to prevent.[2] Moreover,
taking into account the attitude of the uncommitted countries,
any attempt to exploit to the full a chance situation, even
though legally justifiable, would be putting the cohesion of the

[1] See also his speech in the House of Lords on the following day. H.L.
Debs. Vol. 168. Col. 843 (27 July 1950).
[2] 'It is also clear that no enforcement action by the Organization can be
taken against a Great Power itself without a major war. If such a situation
arises the United Nations will have failed in its purpose . . .' Cmd. 6666. *A
Commentary on the Charter of the United Nations*, para. 87. H.M.S.O. 1945.

Organization to a tremendous test, perhaps disrupting it irreparably.

The force of the practical arguments for Communist China's admission was reflected in the Government's policy. When the Korean War had been in progress for nearly six weeks, the British Government again began to support Peking's case in the United Nations. The first move was made in the Security Council on 3 August, but despite the return of the Soviet delegation shortly before, not enough votes could be mustered even to put the matter on the agenda. The opening of a new session of the General Assembly on 19 September presented another opportunity, and from then on Britain gave full backing to the claims of Peking whenever the occasion offered. On 12 October the question was raised in the Economic and Social Council,[1] on 8 November in the Food and Agriculture Organization, and two weeks later was considered by the Trusteeship Council. All Britain's efforts proved useless. In the F.A.O. her proposal to admit a Communist delegate in place of the Nationalist failed even to get a seconder,[2] and in the Trusteeship Council she was the only country to support a similar Soviet motion.[3] The state of American opinion and the paralysing effect upon policy of Congressional elections (the mid-term elections were held in November) made it impossible for the United States to withdraw its opposition, and while the United States stood out, no change of attitude was to be expected from many of the smaller members.

The Korean situation undoubtedly brought a sense of urgency to the whole question as seen from London. In mid-September MacArthur's counter-attack began to sweep all before it. Early in October the Allies crossed the 38th parallel and soon advanced deep into the North. Hitherto China had played no obvious part in the war, but the possibility of her intervention clearly increased with the Allied success. 'I wish to make it clear', said Bevin to the General Assembly on 25 September, 'that we do not intend to break our long-established friendship with China. I can assure the Chinese people that we look forward to the day when they will again take their proper place as

---

[1] *Manchester Guardian*, 13 October 1950.
[2] *New York Herald Tribune*, 9 November 1950.
[3] *Manchester Guardian*, 23 November 1950.

one of the great powers.'[1] The Government was taking a conciliatory line, but whether or not it was hoped that this might
reduce the risk of Chinese intervention, at least it was obvious
that China could not be ignored in the settlement of an affair
which touched her so closely.

Apart, however, from the practical considerations and the
political requirements of a swiftly changing situation, the debate
on the question of China's representation was also carried on in
terms of moral and legal principle. One argument used to
justify the exclusion of Peking was that put forward by Fitzroy
Maclean, a Conservative M.P. and staunch opponent of
Communism, in a letter to *The Times* on 17 November. Maclean
argued that although the Communist Government might control the Chinese people, it was far from being the government
of their choice. Holding Communist China to be a puppet
régime, he maintained that she should be treated as were the
Nazi quisling governments, who naturally were not recognized
by the Allies during the war.

For the parallel to stand, however, the Chinese Communists
would have both to be in complete subjection to Moscow, and
to have been imposed upon a resisting people by outside force.
There was little truth in this as further correspondents pointed
out. Moreover, no one had suggested depriving the Eastern
European governments of their right to be represented at the
United Nations despite the fact that they were far more
obviously Soviet puppets than was the Communist Government
of China.[2]

A second objection of those opposed to the claims of Peking
was that a government of bad or unproven character could not
properly be admitted to an Organization founded upon certain
principles. Although primarily an American argument, it came
to be adopted increasingly on the British Right during the last
months of 1950. 'It is a question', said Lord Salisbury, 'of
whether a nation accepts certain basic standards of conduct for

---

[1] General Assembly, *Official Records, 1950*, Fifth Session, Vol. I, p. 88.

[2] This point was made by Norman Bower in a letter to *The Times* of
21 November 1950. He was one of the few Conservative M.P.s to take a
radical line over China. R. Hamilton, a former Labour M.P., and A. Cun-
ningham Tweedie, also countered the 'puppet' argument in letters of 21
and 22 November and 1 December.

international behaviour.'[1] If it did not, like an unsatisfactory applicant to a club, it was right and proper that it should be black-balled and denied admission.

Whatever the merits of this view, it was difficult to justify in terms of the Charter. For although under Articles 5 and 6 the Charter provided for the suspension or expulsion of members (i.e. states), it said nothing about detaching governments from states and dealing with them separately. Yet this, in effect, was what the opponents of Peking's representation had accomplished by taking advantage of a revolutionary change of government. But why should only revolutionary governments be penalized? The governments of the Soviet Union and of other members had also behaved in ways irreconcilable with certain of the purposes and principles of the Charter. If the ruling was to be of universal application, as in law it should be, why were these suffered to continue to represent their states in the Organization? Admittedly, the existence of an alternative government made China a special case. But this was ensured only by the American protection of Formosa, for it was scarcely conceivable that a few Nationalists in exile would have been permitted to send delegates to the United Nations in the name of China. In fact the whole business savoured of sharp practice. The claims of rival delegations had to be submitted to a credentials committee. But it was the duty of such a committee not to say who ought to represent a member, but simply to decide who did. And the only objective criterion which could be applied was whether the authority sending the delegation exercised effective control over the territory and population of the member state. Even the intervention in Korea against United Nations forces (a ground for suspension under Article 5) was hardly an argument to be employed with any legal relevance unless it was first admitted that Peking was in fact the effective and representative government of China. The proper step then would be to move that China herself should be suspended or expelled from the Organization.[2]

For radicals, however, the bad character of the Chinese Communist Government, even if true, was irrelevant not simply in law but in principle. John Wilkes might be a scoundrel, but

[1] H.L. Debs. Vol. 169. Col. 1001 (14 December 1950).
[2] See G. G. Fitzmaurice, 'Chinese Representation in the United Nations'. *The Year Book of World Affairs, 1952.*

this was no reason to deny the electors of Middlesex the rights of representation. Still less was it right to declare returned his heavily defeated opponent. Leading Liberals and Socialists saw the world as a community of peoples; governments were often left out of consideration.

I take the view [said Lord Addison] that the people of China, as a whole, are a peaceful and peaceably inclined people, and we are more likely ultimately to get on good terms with them by giving facilities for talking over our difficulties with them than by refusing to talk to them at all.[1]

Lord Samuel, in supporting the Communist claim to the Chinese seat, seized upon that rhetorical but somewhat misleading Smutsian opening to the United Nations Charter—'We the Peoples . . .'.[2] Bevin often revealed a like attitude. When, on 14 December, he sought to justify his policy of working for Peking's admission to the United Nations, he said that he could not bring himself to repeat the mistakes of 1917–18 when Russia had been made to feel a nation at bay:

One has to learn lessons from the past, and His Majesty's Government said that if we made a mistake then, we would not commit it again in this case, that we would try not to become obsessed with the Communist conception of China but rather bear in mind that the mass of Chinese scarcely understood what Communism means . . .[3]

In fine, the Chinese seat was the inalienable possession of the Chinese people, and to deprive them of it was to deny them their rightful place in the world community.

Such reasoning, however, was also open to criticism. Few would deny that this right of a people to be represented existed up to a point, but to insist upon it without regard to any other consideration was hardly common sense. Until November 1950 the claims of Peking were supported not only by the main body of Labour and Liberal opinion, but also by leading independent newspapers and journals.[4] Conservatives were for the most part

---

[1] H.L. Debs. Vol. 168. Col. 889 (27 July 1950).

[2] Ibid. Vol. 168. Col. 751 (26 July 1950) and Vol. 169. Col. 1000 (14 December 1950).   [3] H.C. Debs. Vol. 482. Col. 1457.

[4] The Liberal Party Council, meeting on 9 September, urged the Government to press for the transfer of the Chinese seat: *The Times*, 11 September 1950. For press comment see leading articles in *The Times* (7 August), *Manchester Guardian* (3 October) and *Economist* (18 March), and also other articles in the *Economist* (24 June) and *Spectator* (11 August).

silent on the question, but few were hostile and it is likely that without wishing to say so publicly, many of them were of the same mind. For apart from the case for admitting Peking on various practical grounds, it could be held until then, even by those who had little sympathy or respect for it, that the People's Republic of China had been unjustly treated. On 25 October, however, news was received that Chinese Communist forces had begun to invade Tibet, and on 26 November Chinese armies, after earlier reports that they had been taking part in the fighting, launched a major offensive against the United Nations forces in Korea. These developments, however justified by apologists, could not but alter the picture. True, the Charter might have nothing to say about the characters of governments as distinct from states, but was it now a question of upholding the right of John Wilkes to enter Parliament—or Guy Fawkes?

The effect upon the Opposition was immediate. Three days after the start of the Chinese offensive a debate on foreign affairs was held in the House of Commons. In the course of this Eden declared that although the political complexion of Peking was no reason for denying her the Chinese seat, her aggressive conduct was, and for the time being, despite the desirability of having a Chinese Communist spokesman at the United Nations, he failed to see how the Government could continue to press for her admission to an Organization whose forces she was attacking.[1] With the exception of Norman Bower, who had consistently shared the radical view of the question, all the Conservative M.P.s who referred to the subject during the remainder of the year repeated this argument.

One important factor underlying the Tory attitude was undoubtedly dread of appeasement, or what might be construed as appeasement. Lord Salisbury declared on 14 December that to award Peking the Chinese seat when the Chinese were actually fighting the United Nations would be regarded both in the United States and in the Communist world as 'a flagrant example of appeasement out of weakness'.[2] At that moment the Communist armies were not merely fighting the forces of the United Nations, they were driving all before them.

---

[1] H.C. Debs. Vol. 481. Cols. 1178–9 (29 November 1950).
[2] H.L. Debs. Vol. 169. Col. 992.

Munich had shown that concessions made to an opponent flushed with success tend to stimulate rather than mitigate aggressive ambition. The lesson had deeply affected the outlook of many Conservatives, not least, as Suez was later to reveal, the few vindicated by events. The two most strenuous opponents of Peking's admission to the United Nations—Lords Salisbury and Vansittart—had both lost office (the former directly, the latter indirectly) through their opposition to Chamberlain's appeasement policy.[1]

Despite this reaction of the Opposition, the Government held to its policy even when the United Nations forces were in full retreat in Korea. It was not unaware that its motives might be misunderstood,[2] but it believed that apart from the other reasons, if the Korean situation was to be settled under the auspices of the United Nations, it would be better to have Korea's neighbours effectively represented.[3] In fact the Government regarded Peking's occupation of the Chinese seat as the *sine qua non* of a Far Eastern settlement.

In June of the following year, however, came a change of policy. Britain gave up promoting the Communist claim and voted henceforth in favour of deferment. The explanation given was that in existing conditions there was little point in continuing to press for Peking's admission especially as she had persisted in behaviour that was inconsistent with the purposes and principles of the Charter.[4] There was also at this time a general move to bring British policy more into line with that of the United States.[5] Anti-British feeling was then running high in

[1] Salisbury (then Lord Cranborne and Under-Secretary for Foreign Affairs) resigned with Eden in February 1938. Vansittart, Permanent Under-Secretary at the Foreign Office since 1930, was removed by Eden at the end of 1937, his anti-German warnings so irritating the Cabinet as to weaken Eden's influence in it.

[2] Bevin, H.C. Debs. Vol. 482. Col. 1458 (14 December 1950).

[3] Lord Henderson (Under-Secretary for Foreign Affairs) H.L. Debs. Vol. 169. Col. 985 (14 December 1950).

[4] Morrison (Foreign Secretary), H.C. Debs. Vol. 488. Col. 979. (6 June 1951); Younger, Ibid. Cols. *159–60* (11 June 1951).

[5] In May the Government had announced further restrictions upon trade with China, including the suspension of rubber exports: Ibid. Vol. 487. Cols. 1427–32 (3 May 1951), 1589–1600 (7 May) and 2170–88 (10 May). It was also stated that discussion of the future of Formosa would be premature while fighting continued in Korea: Ibid. Cols. 2301–3 (11 May).

America, partly because Britain was widely suspected of having procured MacArthur's dismissal in April, and partly because she had continued to trade with China. Moreover, MacArthur's departure, and perhaps also the resignation shortly after of Aneurin Bevan from the British cabinet, had made possible a greater measure of Anglo–American co-operation in foreign affairs.

Thus, on the question of the Chinese seat the Government had come round to the same view as the Opposition, and when in October the Conservatives were returned to power, they naturally continued to advocate deferment. The new policy, however, proved increasingly unacceptable to important sections of British opinion. Chinese intervention in Korea had not lessened the radical demand for Communist representation in the United Nations. On the contrary, during the crisis of December 1950 when it seemed for a moment that the situation in the Far East would lead to a world war, Peking's admission to the Security Council was regarded by many as an urgent necessity.[1] The crisis passed, but the demand grew. A Gallup poll taken on 20 February 1951 revealed that 40 per cent of those interviewed favoured Peking's admission, 35 per cent being against.[2] The majority, though not large, was shown by later polls to be on the increase. From the following summer an important reason was a growing weariness with the Korean War. With the stabilization of the front to the Allies' advantage, and the opening of armistice talks at the Soviet Government's suggestion, it was difficult any longer to claim that the transfer of the Chinese seat to the People's Republic would be an act of flagrant appeasement. But that it would facilitate a settlement was a view which came increasingly to be held as the armistice talks dragged on through 1952 and into 1953. In Parliament, although it had been the Labour Government which had decided that Britain would give up supporting the Communist claim, Labour M.P.s and former ministers again began to press for Peking's admis-

---

[1] See the letter published in *The Times* on 6 December, signed by a number of politicians, writers, scientists, etc. The majority of them were Socialists, but in a further letter of 8 December, Keith Feiling, the Tory historian, claimed that it would be wrong to think that their views were not shared by many far from the Left.

[2] See Appendix III, B1.

sion, or, if that was not immediately possible, for the expulsion of the Nationalists.[1]

The Conservative Government, however, stuck to its predecessors' policy. It declined to accept the suggestion that the Chinese seat should be declared vacant, holding this to be incompatible with the Charter,[2] nor would it agree that the opinion of the International Court of Justice should be sought.[3] When in July 1953 the Korean armistice was finally negotiated it was widely assumed that the last obstacle to Communist China's admission to the United Nations had been removed. A Gallup poll taken in September revealed that public opinion favoured it in the ratio of 7 to 2, with Conservative opinion having largely swung into line.[4] Yet despite mounting pressure from many quarters, the Government decided, and in so doing caused much dissatisfaction on the Labour benches, that consideration of the problem would have to await the political conference on Korea.[5]

From April to July 1954 representatives of the interested powers met at Geneva for the twofold purpose of arranging a peace settlement for Korea and terminating the conflict in Indo-China. On the first question no progress was made; on the second, the protracted negotiations seemed often to be on the point of breaking down. In Parliament the Opposition maintained that to admit Peking into the United Nations would do much to bring agreement nearer,[6] but the Government held to its line. After returning from a visit he made to the United States early in July, the Prime Minister declared in the Commons that even a satisfactory conclusion to the Geneva Conference would make no difference.[7] And so it proved. On 21 July an agreement was reached bringing peace to Indo-China, but this did nothing to further the cause of Chinese Communist representation and did not in any way affect British policy.

[1] H.C. Debs. Vol. 510. Cols. 200–1 (21 January 1953); Vol. 512. Cols. 815–16 (9 March), 2075–6 (17 March).
[2] Under Articles 23(1) and 28(1). H.C. Debs. Vol. 512. Cols. 815–16 (9 March).   [3] Ibid. Vol. 511. Cols. 392–3 (11 February).
[4] Three Gallup polls show the trend: May—43% to 36%; June—52% to 21%; September—57% to 16%. See Appendix III, B 2–4.
[5] H.C. Debs. Vol. 518. Cols. 1284–6 (29 July 1953).
[6] Attlee, ibid., Vol. 530. Col. 484 (14 July 1954)
[7] Ibid. Col. 46 (12 July 1954).

The main reason for the Government's pursuing this course in face of such widespread criticism at home and despite the fact that the Chinese seat would have proved useful in the bargaining at Geneva, was the unparalleled hostility which would otherwise have arisen in the United States. The visit of Churchill and Eden to Washington in July was proclaimed by Senator Knowland to be an attempt to persuade the Administration to change its mind over the Chinese seat. This caused a furore which amazed even Churchill.[1] Although a Gallup poll taken in Britain in June revealed that 61 per cent of people favoured Peking's admission to the United Nations with only 20 per cent against, the corresponding figures for a poll taken in America during July were 7 per cent in favour, and 78 per cent hostile. Dr. Gallup commented upon this that in the twenty years that the poll had been sampling opinion in the two countries, there have never been an issue which had so divided the two peoples.[2] Indeed, there were many in America who held that the United States should withdraw from the United Nations if Communist China were admitted. The British Government therefore resigned itself to waiting for a change in American opinion, rather than subject Anglo–American relations to the violent strain that a return to its former policy would undoubtedly have caused.

This great difference in Anglo–American opinion should not pass without a word of explanation. The British had never been so emotionally involved in the Korean War as had the Americans. Their military contribution had been much smaller, their casualties far fewer. But apart from this it is characteristic of the Americans that they tend to see all conflict in moral terms. American wars must be struggles of good against evil, the good must triumph and the evil be punished. The Korean War, however, had not ended in victory but in stalemate. This was a unique experience for the Americans who, although capable of swiftly re-establishing friendly relations with an enemy they had chastised, when faced with the existence of an undefeated and impenitent foe could feel only frustration and chagrin. That he had escaped his just deserts was bad enough; that he should

[1] Ibid. Col. 45.

[2] Records of the British Institute of Public Opinion. See Appendix III, B6.

lose nothing for his criminality would be intolerable.[1] The British, with long experience of inconclusive wars, small professional campaigns and the manipulation of the balance of power, felt in the main no such reaction. Although most agreed that an act of aggression could not be allowed to succeed, radical opinion considered that Communist China had at least an arguable case for her intervention, Tory opinion that shots having been exchanged and honour satisfied, there was nothing for it but to shake hands.

Looking at the Chinese seat affair in retrospect, one is struck by the intensity of feeling it aroused and the importance with which it was regarded. Since 1954 interest in the question has waned, and although at the time of writing it is still an unresolved issue, it would be surprising if a disputed representation at the United Nations were ever taken quite so seriously again. The reason for this lies less in the apparent recession of the danger of a major war with an excluded power as in the changes which have occurred in the world political scene since the death of Stalin. When the cold war was at its height, the progressive mutual alienation of East and West, leading perhaps to the horrific vision of George Orwell, seemed to many to be not only a possibility but a probability. The best hope of avoiding this fate seemed to lie in preserving the United Nations as a world institution. Since that time intercourse between Western and Communist powers has steadily increased, with the result that the United Nations is no longer the indispensable rendezvous it once appeared to be. Although the General Assembly, being the place where the smaller and less committed states can raise questions of international concern, shows signs of becoming an embryonic world legislature, it is not in the Security Council, but in the *ad hoc* meetings or consultations of the leaders of the great powers that we might expect to find developing an embryonic world executive.

[1] It is a rule of the American cinema that the lawbreaker never eludes justice.

IV

The Problem of Formosa

The disgust of British opinion for the Nationalist régime and the antipathy with which so many in Britain had viewed American attempts to support a dying and worthless cause, were irritants in Anglo–American relations which by the latter half of 1949 had largely disappeared. For long half-hearted about a policy persisted in largely as a sop to Congressional and public opinion, the Truman Administration seemed finally to have written off the Kuomintang. The Far Eastern crisis which had so far only smouldered, appeared likely to die out. Naturally, it would have taken longer for Washington than for London to establish normal relations with Peking, but the elimination of the Nationalists would have narrowed the field of international tension and probably solved the problem of the Chinese seat.

It soon became apparent, however, that the Chinese civil war would not be so quickly or so conveniently concluded. The Nationalist Government, with the remnants of its forces, withdrew to Formosa, and lacking sea-power the Communists were not immediately able to attack the island. Meanwhile the American Government was subject to growing pressure from military circles and from leading Republican politicians to preserve the Nationalist régime as a permanent threat to Communist stability, and make Formosa a link in the American defence system.

Nothing shows so well the general desire in Britain at this time, even amongst Conservatives, that relations with Communist China should be placed on a regular footing and stability be permitted to return to the Far East, as the outcry which at the start of 1950 greeted the news that the American Government was likely to bow to such pressure.[1] The effect, it

[1] On 29 December 1949 it was announced in Washington that military and civilian advisers would be sent to Formosa, and the Seventh Fleet, based on the Philippines, would be reinforced. Parliament was in recess,

was argued, would be to harm British trade with the mainland, draw China and Russia more firmly together, and risk involving the United States in a major war with Peking. The possibility of the last was almost universally deplored in Britain. Apart from the familiar humanitarian and ideological objections put up for the most part on the Left, there was also the more hard-headed consideration that the more the United States was militarily involved in the Far East, the less she would be able to do for the defence of Western Europe. However, on 5 January 1950, President Truman made it plain that his government had no military interest in Formosa and would keep clear of the civil war even to the extent of refusing to offer advice to the Nationalists.[1] This statement, held to be a victory for Acheson over the military chiefs, was received in Britain with visible relief. On the following day the British Government accorded recognition to Peking.

Little was heard of Formosa during the ensuing months. The Communists had declared their intention of taking it during the course of 1950, and to this the United States Government appeared to be resigned.[2] Had it fallen that spring, there is little doubt that except amongst the American Right the event would have occasioned scarcely more stir in the Western world than the loss of Hainan, the other large island which the Nationalists had hoped to retain, had done in April. The shock of Korea, however, brought a swift change in American policy.

War broke out on 25 June. Only two days later, at the same time as he announced that American forces had been sent to South Korea. President Truman declared that as Communism had passed from subversion to open conquest and had defied the orders of the Security Council, the Communist occupation of Formosa would be a direct threat to the security of the Pacific and to United States forces. Accordingly, the President continued, he had ordered the Seventh Fleet to protect For-

but these proposals were generally attacked in the British press during the first week of 1950. *The Times* and the *Manchester Guardian* in particular carried long critical leading articles on 2 January.

[1] *Documents on International Affairs, 1949–50*, p. 95.

[2] On 12 January 1950 Acheson, in a speech to the National Press Club, declared that Formosa lay outside the American defence zone. As late as 24 May 1950 the American consul-general in Formosa advised Americans to leave. *Survey of International Affairs, 1949–50*, pp. 345–6.

mosa from any mainland attack. But he made it clear to the
Nationalists, after requesting them to stop operations against
the mainland, that the fleet was there to prevent their attacks
also.[1] Formosa had been insulated.

This action by the United States gravely exercised British
opinion, and for the third time in 1950 a development arising
out of the Far Eastern situation threw its shadow over Anglo–
American accord. The British Government, although quick to
associate itself with the steps taken by the President over Korea,
refused to get involved in the Formosa question. No British
help, it was revealed, had been promised to the United States
in the defence of the island, and in the event of a Communist
invasion, the British Far Eastern fleet would remain neutral.[2]
Despite the Korean War and the uncertainty of Communist
intentions, this was simply conforming to a policy already
resolved upon: to do nothing which would materially worsen
relations with Peking or alienate Asian opinion generally.[3]
However, at a time when Anglo–American unity was essential,
the British Government could not afford to be openly critical.

Such criticism as there was at this stage came chiefly from the
Left. Although this was dismissed in some quarters as being
merely the product of the anti-Americanism of certain radical
intellectuals,[4] there was really no more than a half-truth in the
charge. Admittedly those on the Left who had no praise for
President Truman's prompt intervention in Korea found a
better cause for grievance in his Formosa policy, but Formosa
was more than an excuse to work off anti-American or anti-
capitalist feeling. To many Socialists the employment of force in
international politics was still abhorrent. Able to support the
Korean War, at any rate during the early stages, because the
moral principle of opposing aggression was involved, they
nevertheless saw the Seventh Fleet as the instrument of Ameri-

---

[1] *Documents on International Affairs, 1949–50*, p. 632.

[2] See: H.C. Debs. Vol. 477. Cols. 956–7 (10 July 1950); *New York Times*,
quoting an official London source, 21 July 1950.

[3] There was also Hong Kong to consider, the position of which would
have been precarious in the event of a Sino-Western clash over Formosa.
Although it might appear that in such an eventuality Peking would not
have dared to add to its commitments, one has to allow for the notorious
self-confidence of revolutionary regimes.

[4] See: the *Spectator*, 28 July; the *Economist*, 29 July 1950.

can power-politics. Thus in their view it was employed in a role immoral in itself, but made worse by the reactionary nature of the régime being protected. Consequently President Truman's decision to link the two issues, to use Korea as a justification for his action over Formosa, was generally deplored by the heirs of the radical tradition. One Labour M.P. went so far as to table a motion in the House which charged both North Korea and the United States with aggression.[1] The *New Statesman* commented:

By this unilateral act of taking over Formosa, which by universal consent should be returned to China, the Americans have weakened the basis of legality on which they stand, and shown that the underlying issue in the Pacific is the rivalry of two Great Powers.[2]

Indeed, in a letter to the *New Statesman* on 29 July, the veteran Socialist journalist H. N. Brailsford even opposed British participation in the Korean War, claiming that behind the legal façade lay the realities of power-politics. Formosa, he declared, confirmed this.

The opinions of those who expected the world to be all peace and no power—and felt shock and dismay when it turned out otherwise—naturally exasperated those accustomed to think of it as all power and no peace. 'We are under no obligation to hand over Formosa to a hostile China,' declared Lord Vansittart, 'unless we are bent on self-destruction. We are at war with Communism now.'[3] Julian Amery, one of the more prominent of young Tory M.P.s, argued similarly:

Korea and Formosa are not separate issues. They are related military fronts in the world wide struggle between the western nations and the Communist States. . . . The truth is that we are not at peace with the Communist world but at war.[4]

Vansittart, Amery and those of like mind, convinced that the Communists were bent upon world domination (had not Lenin said as much?), took it as axiomatic that everything should be done which could thwart and discomfort them. Amery, who

---

[1] James Hudson, no fellow-traveller but a passionate old radical in the temperance reforming tradition. *The Times*, 30 June 1950.

[2] *New Statesman*, 1 July 1950.

[3] Letter to *The Times*, 26 July 1950.

[4] Letter to *The Times*, 24 July 1950.

F

had declared that given a few atom bombs Chiang Kai-shek might have been saved, argued that Communism in China should be prevented from consolidating as a necessary preliminary to the liberation of the country.[1]

Views such as these, though prevalent in the United States were not widely current in Britain. Opinion about Truman's Formosa policy was at first varied. Some welcomed it, others did not. And the differences to some extent cut across party. Yet upon one point almost all were agreed: that Formosa ought never to be the cause of a major conflict. Many of those supporting the policy of insulation with its ban upon aggression from either side, accepted it indeed as a means of preventing rather than provoking conflict at a time when no one knew whether the Korean War might not spread to other parts. It was because they could not see it in this light but saw instead the awful possibility of World War III developing out of a Sino–American skirmish in the Formosa Straits, that certain others, chiefly though not exclusively of the Left, voiced their apprehensions and desired the British Government to make its position clear.[2] Had Truman enforced a strict impartiality it is unlikely that this uneasiness would have affected more than a few, but following a visit by MacArthur to Chiang Kai-shek early in August, the Nationalists again began to bomb and blockade the mainland. This violation of the Truman declaration was strongly condemned in the British press.[3] Even the *Economist*, usually indulgent to Washington, described MacArthur's visit as being 'calculated to put the very worst possible face upon American policy', and spoke of the 'blundering American diplomacy' which permitted 'such a dangerous situation to arise'.[4]

[1] Article in *The Nineteenth Century and After*, January 1950. Amery was later a 'Suez Rebel'—one of those who baulked not at Eden's starting but at his stopping.

[2] See: letter to *The Times*, 22 July 1950, from Norman Bower, R. H. S. Crossman, J. Grimond and Woodrow Wyatt; *Observer*, leading article, 30 July.

[3] Parliament was in recess, but on 6 August Fenner Brockway, a Labour M.P. on the Left of the Party, sent a telegram to the Prime Minister stressing the danger of war over Formosa. In reply Attlee admitted the peril. *The Times*, 16 August 1950.

[4] *Economist*, 12 and 19 August 1950.

The assumption of those who condemned American policy over Formosa on grounds of its danger to world peace was that a major war could start on the periphery of a power complex and swiftly engage the whole. Thus, any attempt by the Seventh Fleet to destroy Chinese Communist forces in process of invading Formosa would necessarily involve China and the United States in war. Russia, however, would probably be drawn in under the terms of the Sino–Soviet treaty of mutual assistance, and in these circumstances Britain and other Western countries would hardly be likely to escape involvement. Such was the argument. A very different view, however, was that held by Amery:

If Stalin wants war there will be war. If he does not want it he is not going to be provoked into starting it just because the United States have decided to keep Formosa on our side of the barricade.[1]

Which of these interpretations was right? Did the American action over Formosa materially increase the danger of a major conflict or not?

Any government not wholly irresponsible may be presumed to engage upon a war either in the conviction that it will win, or in the realization that, despite the uncertainty of victory, with circumstances changing adversely it is a case of 'now or never', or in the consciousness that owing to domestic or other pressures it is unable to submit to a provocation. How far could these factors be applied to the Communist powers during 1950?

At that time China and Russia could not have fought a total war against the West with any great prospect of success. Indeed, to have attempted to do so would have been to jeopardize the whole Communist experiment. Admittedly both possessed huge armies and on land might have proved invincible, but Chinese air and naval strength was negligible, and in the realm of nuclear weapons the Soviet Union was still three or four years behind the United States. As for a belief that time was running out, this would rarely if ever be entertained by a Communist government, for a Communist sees time as perpetually running in. To be stung into action would also be unlikely in the case of a Communist régime unless it was fully ready to act anyway.

[1] Letter to *The Times*, 24 July 1950.

Thus, on the face of it Amery was right and Left-wing apprehensions were unfounded. Yet fears that the situation might lead to war were not wholly without justification. The ancient Chinese writer on military affairs Sun Wu, laid it down that one should never force an opponent into such desperation that he must leap at one's throat like a rat in a corner. Truman's policy as it stood would not have had this effect, but it is conceivable that if Nationalist activity against the mainland had been resumed, and in consequence of the role of the Seventh Fleet, resumed with impunity, Peking, still far from having fully established its authority, and possibly fearful of the loss of face entailed, would have been forced to safeguard the revolution by taking some drastic and irrevocable step. This might have taken the form of an attempt upon Formosa, despite the Seventh Fleet, or a full-scale intervention in the Korean War at a time when the Allies were hard pressed.[1] Whether the Americans, especially the American militarists, would then have been content with a retaliation that was geographically limited, was by no means certain. Indeed, MacArthur's views upon Formosa were sufficiently removed from the President's for the latter to insist on their being withdrawn after they had been publicly expressed.[2]

In short, there was probably less risk of a great war than the critics of American policy assumed, but rather more than certain of its upholders supposed. Both sides were probably wrong about Russia. Those who criticized American policy saw the Sino–Soviet treaty of mutual assistance as the means by which hostilities between America and China might be transformed into a global cataclysm. But had such a clash occurred over Formosa, Russia would not necessarily have gone to China's aid, for the treaty stipulated only aggression 'by Japan or states

[1] An invasion of Formosa might seem to be out of the question unless Russian air power could have been enlisted, nevertheless there were rumours at the time that the Communists might attempt the job with the aid of thousands of motorized junks, the idea being that the Seventh Fleet could not have sunk them all.

[2] In a message to a veterans' convention on 24 August 1950, MacArthur had spoken of the American ability to dominate every East Asian port, and of the vital place of Formosa in American defence strategy. Truman's disavowal was widely welcomed in Britain.

allied with Japan'[1]—a careful wording which provided the Russians with a loophole. More important than this, even though the fate of Communism in China might have been at stake, for Stalin to have taken so grave a risk with his country's security as to engage in conflict with a power possessed of nuclear superiority, would have been utterly uncharacteristic, a reversal of a policy which he had consistently applied for twenty-five years. On the other hand, the idea favoured by many on the Right that the writ of Stalin ran throughout Communist Asia, and that whether or not a war broke out over Formosa depended upon his will alone, was certainly mistaken. In all probability any Asian Communist movement would want to consult Moscow before taking a decisive step or making an important change of policy, but these movements, being the products of local problems and conditions, were ultimately their own master, and of none was this more true than of Chinese Communism.

When, during the autumn of 1950, the Chinese began to intervene in Korea in strength, most opinion in Britain tended to vere rather more to the American point of view, being concerned only that the island should not become a base for MacArthurian adventures. Certainly, of the two practical alternatives of letting it go or protecting it, protection, at any rate for the duration of the Korean War, seemed to many to be the more prudent and sensible. The Labour Government, too, although not abandoning their view that to interpose the Seventh Fleet between Communists and Nationalists had been a mistake, were nevertheless ready to acknowledge that the Americans had a case. When in December Attlee flew to Washington to discuss the Far Eastern situation with Truman, both agreed that the problem of Formosa should be settled peaceably and in such a way as to safeguard the interests of the inhabitants and the maintenance of peace and security in the Pacific.[2] Although in his memoirs the Prime Minister subsequently revealed that Formosa, like the Chinese seat, was a problem over which he and the President had agreed to differ, and that he himself preferred as a solution the neutralization of the island, it is apparent that the British Government was con-

---

[1] *Documents on International Affairs, 1949–50*, p. 542.
[2] Ibid. p. 124.

tent to let the matter rest.[1] In the debate which followed his visit, Attlee declared that while China continued to intervene in Korea it would be difficult to reach a satisfactory solution.[2] Finally in May 1951, as part of an effort to bring British Far Eastern policy more into line with American,[3] the Foreign Secretary made an unsolicited statement on Formosa in the House of Commons. He declared that it would be premature to discuss the future of the island so long as operations continued in Korea, that it was not the most urgent problem, and that there was no acute friction between Britain and the United States on the matter. Moreover, Formosa would not be allowed to delay the Japanese Peace Treaty which in the opinion of the Government need have nothing to say about a final solution.[4] Accepted by the Conservatives when they took office in October 1951, this remained the official British position throughout the rest of the period covered by this study.

Nevertheless, although the Government might acquiesce, this was by no means true of the whole country. There were some, a minority perhaps but vociferous, who remained highly critical of the whole Western handling of the Formosa problem, even after the Chinese had attacked and thrown back the West in Korea. Naturally the voices of Communists and fellow-travellers were added here, but these are not our concern.

In general those who attacked American policy on Formosa were the same as those who upheld Peking's claim to the Chinese seat in the United Nations. In their opinion Communist China had certain legitimate grievances which caused her to behave belligerently; as for the West, in its treatment of China it had fallen below those standards of integrity and fair dealing which it purported to uphold. Such criticism, so far as Formosa was

---

[1] C. R. Attlee. *As It Happened*, p. 201. The American policy was often referred to as 'neutralization' but it is evident from his later pronouncements that by this the Prime Minister meant the disarming of the Nationalists and the placing of Formosa under an international guarantee. It could not then be considered a threat to the security of either side.

[2] H.C. Debs. Vol. 482. Cols. 1354–5 (14 December 1950).

[3] See above, p. 63.

[4] Morrison, H.C. Debs. Vol. 487. Cols. 2301–3 (11 May 1951). In the Peace Treaty, concluded September 1951, Japan merely renounced her sovereignty over Formosa and the Pescadores Islands; no mention was made of their transfer to any government.

concerned, centred particularly upon a supposed failure to implement the Cairo Declaration of 1943.

Formosa had been vaguely part of the Chinese Empire from 1683 until first administered as a province in 1887. A few years later it was ceded to Japan as a result of the Japanese victory in the war of 1894–5. At the Cairo Conference of 1943, Roosevelt, Churchill and Chiang Kai-shek declared that after Japan had been defeated all territory that she had formerly taken from China would be restored. This was reaffirmed at Potsdam, and in 1945, with Allied sanction, Formosa was occupied and administered by the Chinese. When, therefore, the Communists took possession of the mainland of China, but were prevented by the Seventh Fleet from obtaining Formosa, the American action was held by a number of its critics to have amounted to the dishonouring of a promise. Lord Stansgate, a fit representative of old-style radical integrity, commented:

The Cairo Declaration said that Formosa should be given back to China. The Chinese are now asking to have it back and we say, 'Because you are Communists we are not going to keep our word'. If we say that our plighted word depends on the interests of State, we are adopting one of the fundamental principles of the Communist faith.[1]

The lawyers might object that the Declaration was merely a unilateral statement of intent which only the peace treaty could make valid, and that in any case it was a matter of opinion whether or not 'China' possessed the island already; realists might dismiss with impatience a scrupulousness which however much an asset in the days of Gladstone or Edward Grey would to many seem laughable or pathetic in the changed circumstances of 1950; yet even in a more cynical age, a charge against the national honour, even though the fault lay merely in condoning what another had done, was not lightly to be dismissed, especially by that small but still influential section

[1] H.L. Debs. Vol. 171. Col. 658 (2 May 1951). See also: *New Statesman*, 1 July 1950; Lord Strabolgi, H.L. Debs. Vol. 168. Col. 779 (26 July 1950), Vol. 170. Col. 762 (1 March 1951); letter from A. J. P. Taylor, *The Times*, 26 July 1950; T. Driberg, H.C Debs. Vol. 481. Col. 1384 (30 November 1950); G. A. Pargiter, ibid. Vol. 482. Col. 1413 (14 December 1950); Lord Silkin, H.L. Debs. Vol. 169. Col. 1017 (14 December 1950); letter from Sir John Pratt, *Manchester Guardian*, 22 December 1950.

of British people that was later to regard the Suez Affair as one of the most sordid exploits in recent British history. It was there-fore fortunate—at least in the interest of Anglo–American rela-tions—that the insulation of Formosa could be defended on grounds which no liberal or radical could altogether ignore: namely humanitarian.

During the course of 1950, it became apparent that the Com-munist revolution was by no means as bloodless as earlier reports had made out. Indeed, the Communists themselves admitted that they had proceeded to the liquidation of their enemies and shot large numbers of people.[1] Clearly, therefore, to permit a Communist invasion of Formosa would be tanta-mount to condemning thousands of Nationalists to execution, particularly as the island was the last refuge of those who had most to fear. The upholders of the American action repeatedly stressed this aspect. Lord Vansittart declared that Formosa should be withheld from China not because the Chinese were Communists, but because they were 'brutes', and because a change of rule would be followed by mass butcheries.[2] A little later the *Economist* put the point neatly when it remarked that those who would like to see Formosa in the hands of Peking had yet to suggest a place to which Chiang Kai-shek and his 600,000 followers might migrate.[3] Churchill, too, when as prime minister he addressed a joint session of Congress during his visit to Washington at the beginning of 1952, confined him-self, when touching upon Formosa, to the argument that was likely to cause the least trouble at home.

---

[1] *Survey of International Affairs, 1951*, p. 372. One authority regarded as a conservative estimate a total of 3,000,000 to 5,000,000 executions in the first two years of Communist rule. See Kenneth Scott Latourette, *A History of Modern China*, p. 213. Most Western commentators, however, have quoted the figure of 2,000,000 for executions during 1950–52. This was derived from official Chinese statements, but whether it referred actually to execu-tions depends upon how the word 'liquidated' should be interpreted. Some observers—and not only apologists like Ralph and Nancy Lapwood, *Through the Chinese Revolution*, pp. 144–6, and Peter Townsend, *China Phoenix: The Revolution in China*, pp. 373–80—have claimed that it meant no more than 'dealt with'. Nevertheless even Townsend assumed that 'quite considerable numbers' of executions must have taken place (p. 380).

[2] H.L. Debs. Vol. 171. Col. 692 (2 May 1951).

[3] *Economist*, 18 August 1951.

I am very glad [he declared] that whatever diplomatic divergencies there may be from time to time about the procedure, you do not allow the Chinese anti-Communists on Formosa to be invaded and massacred from the mainland.[1]

In fact there was little to choose between the Communists and the Nationalists on the score of inhumanity. As Michael Lindsay and the *New Statesman* pointed out, Nationalist rule in Formosa itself had been marked by repressions and massacres following the unrest provoked by chronic misgovernment.[2] Certainly the bad character of the Kuomintang had never been forgotten or ignored in liberal and radical circles, yet once news of the Communist executions became known, there was a growing unwillingness, except amongst a minority chiefly of the Left, that Formosa should be left to its fate. The reason for this seems to be that opinion in countries without experience of tyranny or misrule invariably sympathizes with the victims or potential victims of revolutionary retribution, rarely considering that this itself is usually a type of rough justice and that an escape from it may amount to a denial of justice. In Britain, at any rate, the Scarlet Pimpernel will always be a hero.[3]

However, as far as the safeguarding of human life is concerned, irrespective of who was saved and at what risk to world peace, the policy of insulation would appear to have had much to commend it. Many thousands of Nationalists escaped the firing squads; civilians on the mainland were largely spared the effects of futile and indiscriminate raids by Nationalist aircraft; and Chiang Kai-shek's 600,000 men were ensured against the slaughter that would inevitably have accompanied any foolhardy attempt by their leaders to stage a come-back. On the other hand it could be argued that but for the existence of a

---

[1] *Documents on International Affairs, 1952*, p. 49.

[2] See: letter from Michael Lindsay, *Manchester Guardian*, 11 July 1950; *New Statesman*, 12 August 1950. In 1947 some 5,000 Formosans were killed by Nationalist troops following a rebellion provoked by the oppressions and exactions of the Kuomintang governor. See the American White Paper, *United States Relations with China* (1949), Annex 169.

[3] The alternative point of view was brought home to the writer in an amusing way. Mention being made in conversation of Baroness Orczy's famous tale, a young West Indian Communist who was present declared that it was a tenth-rate novel by a tenth-rate novelist. His objection was not a literary one, but that the book glorified the rescue of reactionaries from the just vengeance of the progressives.

rival government on Formosa, and the consequent fear that with foreign help it would seek to re-establish itself, the Terror which swept China during the first year of the Korean War and in which perhaps as many as two million former Nationalist supporters lost their lives, either would have been much less severe or would not have taken place.

Many of those who disliked and distrusted the Kuomintang, who even thought that the Communists had a case, but who were fearful enough of Communist intentions not to want to see the island fall prey to Peking, took refuge in the idea that the Formosans had a right to self-determination. This solution appealed particularly to members of the Liberal Party, the right of a people to choose its own government and decide its own destiny being classic liberal doctrine.[1] It was not, however, one which found favour with those who were convinced of the essential justice of Peking's claim, any more than the related suggestion that Formosa should be made a ward of the United Nations. The idea of a plebiscite met with some telling opposition in Parliament. Would the British people, declared Lord Chorley, consent to a plebiscite in Kent and Essex if those counties had earlier been taken from them?[2] Another Labour peer, Lord Strabolgi, cited the precedent of Alsace-Lorraine in 1919 when there was never any doubt in French minds about its return and no question of a plebiscite.[3] Lord Ailwyn, a Unionist, thought the idea illogical because it had been suggested only when the Communists had come to power in China; nothing, he maintained, was said about the wishes of the Formosans after the Cairo or Potsdam Declarations.[4]

If we adopt the liberal view that the right of self-determination exists, we have to balance it against the right of the state to preserve its integrity. For to admit the right of any village, town or petty province to opt for independence or transfer to

---

[1] See: J. Grimond, H.C. Debs. Vol. 484. Col. 75 (12 February 1951); Lord Perth ('Although apparently self-determination is rather out of favour, as a Liberal I find it is the right method of settling difficulties of this kind.'), H.L. Debs. Vol. 171. Col. 634 (2 May 1951); *News Chronicle*, leading article, 12 May 1951.

[2] H.L. Debs. Vol. 170. Cols. 710–1 (28 February 1951).

[3] Ibid. Vol. 170. Col. 762 (1 March 1951), Vol. 171. Cols. 644–5 (2 May 1951).   [4] Ibid. Vol. 170. Col. 773 (1 March 1951).

another's rule would be to admit anarchy. When, however, we turn for guidance to historical examples, we find that liberals, and especially American liberals, have approached self-determination almost entirely in terms of the struggle of minorities against imperialism. Thus the Irish, the Poles, the Italians, and all the subject peoples of the Hapsburg and Ottoman Empires were accredited with a right of which the American South was forcefully dispossessed and which the American Indians or Negroes were never regarded as having. In other words, the right of self-determination as traditionally understood and upheld by Western liberals, would appear to depend upon the fulfilment of certain conditions. First, the minority should have a distinct ethnic, linguistic or religious character. Secondly, it must be geographically compact so as to form an undoubted majority in a particular area. Thirdly, it should live under sufficient disabilities for its claim to independence to be a reasonable one. Fourthly, the will to independence must be clearly manifested. Granted these conditions, with the possible addition of a fifth, that the minority in question should live in someone else's country, and a *prima facie* claim to self-determination might be said to have been established.

In the light of these tests, however, it is debatable whether this right could fairly be substantiated in the case of Formosa. Admittedly the island has an aboriginal population, but the overwhelming majority of its inhabitants are Chinese or of Chinese descent. Moreover, although they were badly governed in the early years of Kuomintang administration, so was nearly everybody else, and there is no reason to suppose, presuming that they were again to come under the control of the mainland, that they would fare any differently from the bulk of the Chinese people. It is probable that the Communist invasion and attempted subjection of Tibet had something to do with the movement of opinion in favour of self-determination for Formosa, but unlike Formosa, Tibet is pre-eminently a case in which self-determination would appear to be justified.[1]

---

[1] On the other hand it could be argued that, having for so long been subject to an alien rule and education, and having in consequence developed a distinct cultural character and a much higher standard of living than obtained on the mainland, the Formosans, irrespective of the interests of the Nationalists, had at least the basis of a case for separate statehood.

Obviously, these objections apply only if it is first conceded that Formosa is fully a part of metropolitan China. From the strictly legal point of view the island's status since the Japanese peace treaty may be held to be indeterminate, sovereignty having been renounced but not transferred. To make this the plea for advocating self-determination, however, is to hang one's case upon a thread of legal gossamer.[1] On 30 August 1945 the Chinese Government formally proclaimed Formosa a province of China. That this is what she remains is one thing at least upon which both Communists and Nationalists agree.

It was not, however, these moral and legal considerations, but any sign or hint that with American help Chiang Kai-shek might attempt to invade the mainland, that most disturbed opinion in Britain. The first and perhaps worst alarm, that which was occasioned by MacArthur's visit to Formosa in August 1950 and the subsequent Nationalist activity, we have already noticed, but similar incidents and indiscretions continued to arouse apprehension until nearly the end of the Korean War.

On 21 January 1951, Ernest Gross, deputy United States delegate to the United Nations, declared that his country reserved the right to handle the Formosa question in a way consistent with American interests and security. Although Gross's speech was played down by the State Department it made a bad impression in Britain, being described by *The Times* correspondent as distressing and embarrassing to America's allies.[2]

Three months later Acheson revealed that in February the American Government had agreed to arm the Nationalists and send a military mission to Formosa to supervise their training.[3] This provoked but little immediate criticism, probably because the news followed shortly after MacArthur's dismissal. On 18

---

[1] Even before the Japanese treaty, the official British view that Formosa was not legally Chinese was open to several legal objections (see article by L. C. Green in the *International Law Quarterly* for July 1950, pp. 418–22). After the treaty, to claim that the island's status was indeterminate was almost as legally pedantic as to maintain that East Prussia is still German for lack of a German peace treaty.

[2] See: *The Times*, 23 and 24 January; *New York Herald Tribune*, 28 January 1951.

[3] *Survey of International Affairs, 1951*, p. 353.

May however, Dean Rusk, Assistant Secretary of State for Far Eastern Affairs, said in Washington that the Administration would continue to aid the Nationalist Government which 'more authentically represented the views of the great body of the people of China' than did Peking.[1] At once a storm of protest burst in Britain. Not only was Rusk's speech widely condemned in the press, but the Foreign Office was so concerned that it took the unusual step of sending the Ambassador, Sir Oliver Franks, to the State Department for an explanation.[2] Acheson, when he heard of the speech was said to have been 'hopping mad',[3] and quickly issued a denial that a change of policy was imminent. British uneasiness, however, was not entirely dispelled. The *Observer*, for example, on 12 August 1951 commented:

It must be hoped that America will retain effective control over the use to which Generalissimo Chiang Kai-shek puts the arms now placed in his hands, and not allow this very dubious ally, who has already wasted two billion United States dollars on forlorn ambitions, to start new adventures of his own. The purpose for which he is to be armed is the defence of Formosa, not, emphatically, the invasion of China.

In the following year another speech by an American official seemed to show that these were no longer the views of Washington. On 1 April 1952, when the Nationalists were better armed and organized, Dan Kimball, the United States Secretary for the Navy, after a visit to Formosa advocated increased aid and declared that if the Nationalists invaded the mainland, the United States Navy would 'stand on the sidelines and cheer'.[4] Again the State Department disassociated itself, but the speech was ill-received in Britain, especially by the Labour press.

Finally, on 30 January 1953, President Eisenhower suddenly announced that the Seventh Fleet would no longer prevent a Nationalist attack upon the mainland, but only a Communist invasion of Formosa. The British Government immediately protested at this change of policy by the new Republican Administration. On 3 February Eden announced in the House of Commons:

[1] Ibid.   [2] *New York Herald Tribune*, 23 May 1951.
[3] *The Times*, Washington correspondent, 23 May 1951.
[4] *Manchester Guardian*, 2 April 1952.

Her Majesty's Government were informed in advance by the United States Government, and at once made known their concern at this decision—(cheers)—which they feared would have unfortunate political repercussions without compensating military advantages. (cheers) This continued to be the view of the British Government.[1]

Opposition leaders also expressed grave concern, asking for and being granted, a special debate. One Labour member even suggested that the Royal Navy should take on the job of confining Chiang Kai-shek to his island.[2] The press, too, was largely critical, and the Peace with China Council, about which little had been heard since the recall of MacArthur, was again stirred into activity.[3]

Although Eisenhower's decision was really made to placate Republican opinion at home and possibly to force the Chinese to withdraw some of their forces from Korea, there is little doubt that the extreme touchiness of British opinion on the subject of a Nationalist come-back helped to prevent the Americans from doing anything rash. At least the fact that the United States' major ally would in all probability stand aside from a Sino–American conflict over Formosa, must have provided a useful argument for those counselling moderation in Washington.[4]

[1] *The Times*, 4 February 1953.
[2] H.C. Debs. Vol. 510. Cols. 1672–8 (3 February 1953).
[3] See Appendix II.
[4] No poll of British opinion on the Formosa question was taken until January 1955, after the conclusion of the period covered by this study. But a poll taken in that month shows a substantial majority in favour of British neutrality if such a conflict should arise. See Appendix III, C1.

V

The Korean War: *The First Phase*

Unlike the problems of the Chinese seat and Formosa, the Korean War was not, as a whole, a subject of contention between British and American opinion. Prevailing sentiment in both countries was at one in acknowledging the necessity both of resisting aggression and of doing so under the aegis of the United Nations. Yet not only was the impact of the war upon the two countries very different, but below the overriding solidarity that both maintained to the end, the arguments and controversies almost inseparable from Anglo–American involvement in Far Eastern affairs were given plenty of scope during the three years that the conflict lasted.

At the beginning, however, all was singleness of purpose. Indeed, rarely has Britain been so united, both within itself and with its Allies, as during the opening phase of the Korean War. This is the more remarkable when it is remembered that a large section of Left-wing opinion had always expressed sympathy for the new revolutionary régimes of Asia, whether Communist or not, and that over three important Far Eastern issues the Government, and with it much of the country, had been in sharp disagreement with the United States. Moreover, the North Korean attack upon South Korea early in the morning of 25 June 1950 was to the world at large as enigmatic as it was sudden. Ostensibly it was simply a struggle between the ideologically opposed halves of a small artificially divided country. But were there wider implications? Behind North Korea there was the Chinese Red Army with its millions of well-disciplined, newly victorious veterans, and in the background the recently acquired Soviet atomic bomb. Would the North Koreans have dared to move without authorization from Moscow, and in the event of Western intervention was it not likely that China, and perhaps Russia also, had agreed to come to their aid? Or was the idea one of getting the West entangled in a side-show so that Europe or the Middle East would be left the more vulnerable to Russian pressure? Considerations such as these might well have induced caution on the part of the Government, or have evoked widespread opposition to any move likely to increase the risk of a major war. Instead the British cabinet, like the American president, promptly declared for intervention and in so doing earned the almost unanimous support of Parliament as well as the backing of the great mass of opinion in the country.

This response was in large part a reflex action born of the experience of the previous twenty years. Naturally the security of Japan and its immediate neighbourhood meant far less to the British than it did to the Americans. The crisis was upon the other side of the world and British interests were not immediately involved. Moreover, the Americans had made the Far East their own rather jealously guarded preserve, and thus the feeling that they should do what needed doing themselves—the more so that Britain had sufficient to cope with in Malaya— was understandable enough. For these reasons public opinion had at first been hesitant.[1] But quickly the seriousness of the situation, the preparedness of the Communists, the impotence of their opponents, and the possibility that Korea was being deliberately used to test Western reactions, became apparent. Was Korea, in fact, to be the Communist 'occupation of the Rhineland'? The nation had come far since Chamberlain had bemoaned the digging of trenches and trying on of gas-masks 'because of a quarrel in a far-away country between people of whom we know nothing'.[2] It was the obvious public disgust for the apathy and appeasement of the 1930s and for the neglect and blindness which had characterized government policy during those years—the full story of which had been newly revealed to millions through the publication in 1948 of the first volume of Churchill's war memoirs—that made the cabinet confident that it could carry the country with it in deciding to go to war over Korea.[3]

---

[1] This attitude was noted in the leading article of the *Economist*, 1 July 1950. The Beaverbrook press at first adopted an isolationist line. The editorial of the *Evening Standard* of 26 June was headed: 'We are not involved'.

[2] Keith Feiling, *The Life of Neville Chamberlain*, p. 372.

[3] Kenneth Younger, 'Public Opinion and Foreign Policy'. *The British Journal of Sociology*, Vol. VI, No 2. (June 1955), p. 171.

This alone, however, does not account for the high degree of support for intervention. Suez, too, was largely the product of the anti-appeasement reaction, yet it raised fierce antagonisms and divided the country. The reason why the action taken over Korea had no such effect was that, unlike Suez, it did not outrage the liberal and radical moral conscience. The North Koreans, whatever case they might have had against Syngman Rhee and his reactionary despotic government, and even supposing that their decision was prompted solely by provocation, had put themselves hopelessly in the wrong by resorting to war. It was 'naked aggression and must be checked', declared Attlee on 27 June,[1] but whereas the Right would probably have welcomed intervention even if it had been only national—as it did in later years over Suez, the Lebanon and Jordan—that it was proceeded with in the name and at the request of the United Nations ensured also the support of all but the extremists of the Left. That at last the hopes that so many had held of the League were being fulfilled was something which appealed strongly to liberal and radical sentiment—especially in the first flush when the undertaking looked like being truly international rather than, as was soon apparent, an American operation with international dressing. In Labour circles particularly, the belief that the League had been 'let down' by cynical reactionaries who had regarded it with barely concealed contempt, and that the rot had begun with failure to mobilize the nations against aggression in this very quarter of the world in 1931, was widely prevalent. We must remember the lesson of Manchuria and the League, said Attlee,[2] and for a short while something approaching enthusiasm was shown for the League's apparently more effective successor.

Those who condemned the course taken by the British Government were comparatively few, being almost without exception either pacifists or adherents of the extreme Left. The objections raised were various. Some considered that the Security Council, by taking action in the absence of Russia—the Soviet delegation was still boycotting proceedings over the issue of the Chinese seat—had behaved illegally.[3] Others saw fault in the steps lead-

[1] H.C. Debs. Vol. 476. Col. 2161.
[2] Ibid. Vol. 477. Col. 493 (5 July 1950).
[3] See the *New Statesman*, 8 July 1950, London Diary and Correspondence.
G

ing to the Allied intervention, particularly Truman's decision to send forces into battle a few hours before such a move had been authorized by the Security Council. Declared Henry Usborne in the House of Commons:

. . . we are clearly supporting an armed intervention which was initiated in advance of the collective decision of the body which made the law and that demonstrates the absurdity of the position.[1]

The implication that the United States had acted outside the Charter or infringed international law was refuted by the Government. International law recognized, declared the Prime Minister, the right of any state to defend itself and the right of any other state to assist; this was acknowledged by Article 51 of the Charter.[2] In fact the complaint was pedantic. Truman may appear to have anticipated the second Security Council resolution, but clearly the first, which besides calling upon the North Koreans to withdraw, required member states to render every assistance to the United Nations in executing the order, was sufficient justification for his action.[3] These legal objections, however, whether that the Security Council or that the United States had acted *ultra vires*, scarcely merit a detailed legal rejoinder, at any rate in this study. For in general it was less the law than the events which worried the Left-wing critics. Either they disliked a resort to force, even in answer to force, or their sympathies lay more with North Korea than with South. The worst of it was that North Korea was so patently the aggressor. This had been enough to ensure a very wide measure of support for the Anglo–American policy throughout the Labour movement. The National Council of Labour, representing the Labour Party, the Trade Unions and the Co-operative movement, fully upheld the Security Council's action.[4] The Trades Union Con-

---

[1] Usborne (Labour), H.C. Debs. Vol. 476. Col. 2294 (28 June 1950).

[2] Attlee, ibid. Vol. 477. Col. 492 (5 July 1950). Article 51 applies only to member states, but South Korea, if not a member of the Organization, was nevertheless its creation.

[3] The first resolution was approved during the afternoon of 25 June, the day of the attack. At noon on 27 June, Truman announced that as North Korea had ignored the Security Council's demand, American naval and air forces had been ordered to support the South in conformity with the resolution. Three hours later a second resolution was passed requesting members to furnish aid.   [4] *The Times*, 29 June 1950.

gress voted in favour of it by an overwhelming majority.[1] The Parliamentary Labour Party, with but few exceptions, on the main issue stood solidly behind the Government. Even *Tribune*, a journal voicing the opinions of those who later came to be known as Bevanites, commented on 30 June '. . . the United States Government has, in our view, taken the correct and inevitable course'. The dissentients, therefore, having grudgingly to admit that North Korea ought not to have done it, found in the possible legal irregularities a less controversial basis for attacking Western policy than their own ethical or ideological predilections. If the aggressor had been Franco Spain, and if the French delegation, perhaps through the fall of a government, had not been present to exercise an expected veto, it is difficult to imagine any objections to Security Council action being made by the same Left-wing legalists.

Some of the attitudes and prejudices underlying the opposition to intervention were revealed in the debate on Korea held in the House of Commons on 5 July 1950.[2] To the Prime Minister's motion of support for the Government's action, two Welsh Labour members, S. O. Davies and Emrys Hughes,[3] moved the following amendment:

This House expresses its deep concern at the alarming situation in Korea, and recognizes the possibility of another world conflict arising therefrom. It therefore calls upon the Government to withdraw all British naval forces from the affected area; to give full recognition to the claim of the Korean people for the unification and independence of their country; to repudiate all British commitments which involve on our part any obligations to maintain the present division of the nations of the world into two powerful and dangerously poised hostile groups; and to declare, in conformity with the Government's Socialist principles, our determination to give every encouragement to all peoples aspiring to freedom and self-government.[4]

After an attack on Churchill, whom he described as 'never so

---

[1] On 6 September the T.U.C. approved the United Nations intervention in Korea by 6,942,000 to 595,000 votes. *The Times*, 7 September 1950.

[2] H.C. Debs. Vol. 477. Cols. 485–596.

[3] That Davies and Hughes were Welsh may be more than coincidental. One would expect the Welsh to be more sensitive than the English about great power interference in the affairs of a small country.

[4] H.C. Debs. Vol. 477. Cols. 545–6.

happy as when all hell in terms of war is let loose', Davies went on to express his regret that the Government should have aligned itself with the 'corrupt regime of Syngman Rhee' and allowed itself 'to be drawn into this tragic situation by the wholly irregular action of the U.S.A.' He then declared that the American action was 'in direct violation of the letter and spirit of the United Nations Charter', and added:

I should have expected a Socialist Government to be a little more deliberate and cool-headed in such a situation as this and not to have plunged headlong in support of the reckless irresponsibility of the United States. . . . Had it not been for the unprovoked aggression of the United States, . . . this conflict would have finished in a week.[1]

In seconding the motion, Emrys Hughes, a veteran pacifist and son-in-law of Keir Hardie, chiefly concerned himself with the danger of a third world war.

These speeches, particularly that of Davies, brought forth continual protests and interruptions, especially from the Opposition. A Labour member declared that neither Davies nor Hughes was representative of the British working class, and a Conservative commented that they spoke for nobody but 'their two addle-pated selves'. Certainly they spoke only for themselves in the House, and their amendment was rejected without a division, yet similar views were shared by a small, vociferous minority in the country. In an editorial headed 'The Appeasers', the *Manchester Guardian* on 24 July remarked that whereas from 1935 to 1938 it was the Right which refused to see any issue of principle or threat to world peace in aggression, now it was a section of the Left. This anti-American fringe, it added, professing to be devoted to the United Nations, shrank from supporting any decisions that meant action. Five days later the *Economist* commented that appeasement was being voiced 'from a quarter where it is an article of faith that nothing the capitalist Americans do can be wholly right'. This broadly was true. Dislike of America was the emotive force in Left-wing British neutralism as anti-colonialism was in Asian. Hence the fact of North Korean aggression was practically dismissed as irrelevant, the outbreak being primarily regarded as a heaven-sent opportunity for the American militarists, arms

[1] Ibid. Cols. 548 and 550.

manufacturers, war profiteers, China Lobby, and all other elements whom a thoroughgoing Socialist would find anathema, to achieve their ends. Clearly the British Government had played into the hands of the unholy alliance of MacArthur, Syngman Rhee and Chiang Kai-shek, and as for the United Nations, was this not in danger of becoming another Delian League, such as was formed to protect Hellas from an aggressive Oriental despotism, but which ended as the instrument of Athenian imperialism?[1] This, however, was only part of the case against intervention. As with China, so with South Korea: the supplanting of the existing order by Communism was looked upon, if not exactly as the triumph of light over darkness, then certainly as a change which on balance was very much to be desired. Our sympathies, wrote K. Zilliacus[2] in a letter to the *New Statesman* on 8 July, should lie with native Communism as against American-imposed capitalism. A similar sentiment was later expressed by the Socialist intellectual, Professor G. D. H. Cole:

I wanted the North to win. The Government of South Korea appeared to me to be a hopelessly reactionary puppet affair. I do not like Communism; but I like even less reactionary landlordism backed by foreign force against the will of the people.[3]

These views were not likely to win general acceptance amongst those who took a similar line over China, and for two reasons. First, there was no evidence that the North Korean régime represented 'the will of the people' any more than did the South Korean. Set up under Soviet military occupation, it resembled more the satellite régimes of Eastern Europe than it did the Chinese Communist which was truly native and, in the sense that it was the only alternative to anarchy, even popular. Second, whereas the Chinese revolution was basically a great elemental upheaval, the last act of a process which had started long before the arrival of Communism, the Korean

---

[1] See the letter from Edward Hyams, *New Statesman*, 15 July 1950.

[2] Zilliacus, a former Labour M.P., was one of the half dozen expelled from the Labour Party in 1949 for continued criticism of the Government's foreign policy. He was readmitted in 1952 and re-entered Parliament in 1955.

[3] From 'As a Socialist Sees It' by G. D. H. Cole, *New Statesman*, 3 February 1951.

conflict, begun deliberately, and involving the rival protégés of
the Soviet Union and the United States, was more directly and
more immediately related to the contest between Moscow and
Washington for power and prestige in the Far East. Victory for
North Korea would have meant not merely the local resolving
of an unsatisfactory and unstable situation, but an enhance-
ment of Soviet prestige and influence throughout Asia and a
corresponding humiliation for the United States. Furthermore
the United Nations would have been discredited, perhaps
fatally, and encouragement given to all who had so far desisted
from resorting to force through fear of the consequences. This
consideration seems to have weighed little with the opponents
of intervention, but then they had rated the crime of aggression
—technical aggression they would have called it—far lower than
that of reaction. In an age when world stability seemed to
matter as never before, at any rate to the West, this was an
unfashionable view to take. Moreover they spoilt their case
by rounding upon the Americans, not when MacArthur was
advancing triumphantly to the Yalu, but when his few scattered
forces, fighting against formidable odds, were being harried
down the peninsula. Such a display at such a time was unlikely
to appeal to the sporting instincts of the British people.

For one notable critic of intervention the North Korean
aggression presented no difficulty: it had simply never occurred.
The story that the South Koreans had attacked first was put
out by the North Korean Government almost immediately
and was at once accepted throughout the Communist world.
Had it been dismissed by everybody else it would hardly be
worth mentioning, but the charge was later taken up and
elaborated by one of Britain's leading experts on the Far East.
Sir John Pratt[1] held that the United States Government had
encouraged Syngman Rhee to bolster his declining political
prestige by attempting the conquest of the North with his
American-trained army. The attack, he maintained, was

---

[1] Born 1876. From 1906 to 1925 he held various consular posts in China
including those of Consul-General at Nanking and at Shanghai. Acting
Counsellor at the Foreign Office, 1929–38. Head of Far East Section
Ministry of Information, 1939–41. Foreign Office representative, Universities China Committee, and Vice-Chairman, Governing Body of the School
of Oriental and African Studies, at the time of the Korean War.

launched early on the morning of 25 June, but within a few hours the invaders had been thrown back by the North Korean counter-offensive. The United States Government had deliberately distorted the telegram on the origin of the war sent by the United Nations Commission from Seoul. Furthermore, he continued, MacArthur had needed the war as an excuse to seize Formosa. The British Government knew the facts, but to their shame kept quiet.[1]

These sinister accusations, although they delighted the Communists, coming as they did from a non-Communist observer of high standing, appear to have made little impression otherwise, except possibly upon those whose credulity was equalled only by their partiality. To most minds the immediate and powerful advance of the North Koreans told its own tale. Whether there was any basis of fact behind the alternative version of the affair it is impossible to say. The conclusion given in the *Survey of International Affairs* for 1949–50, after a detailed examination of the whole problem, was that in the absence of further evidence the Communist story of a South Korean attempt to conquer the North must be rejected.[2]

Nevertheless the frontier had been a troubled one, and it is possible that a South Korean raid was in progress during the early hours of 25 June and that this circumstance was utilized by North Korean propaganda. Two further considerations, overlooked in the *Survey*, may be mentioned here. First, if a South Korean offensive had in fact been launched before dawn, the evidence of aggression to be found in the presence of the invading troops upon North Korean soil would have been of such incalculable diplomatic advantage that no government in its senses would have thrown it away for the doubtful satisfaction of expelling the attackers before breakfast. Second, in its account of the day's happenings the United Nations Commission on Korea reported that a North Korean sea-borne force had landed on the east coast some thirty miles south of the Parallel—and presumably much farther from the port of em-

---

[1] For reports of meetings addressed by Sir John Pratt, see the *Scotsman*, 10 and 19 December 1951 and 4 February 1952; see also his article published in the *Daily Worker*, 24 October 1951, and his pamphlet *Korea: The Lie that led to War* (1951).

[2] *Survey of International Affairs, 1949–50*, pp. 471–7.

barkation—as early as 6 a.m.[1] If this was true, and in contrast to anything which may have taken place along the Parallel before daybreak it should have been simple enough to verify, it meant that a North Korean invasion was under way by the previous evening at the latest. This would preclude the possibility, in any case highly improbable, that the North Korean offensive was the direct result of a South Korean attack.

It does not follow from this that Sir John Pratt was necessarily wrong in his contention that Syngman Rhee had intended to invade the North, or had even had American encouragement to do so. Clearly Rhee would have made the attempt if confident of success, and equally clearly in certain American quarters there would have been a willingness to let him try. But this is beside the point. As far as United Nations intervention is concerned, the actual responsibility for the aggression of 25 June alone is relevant, and in making his views public Sir John Pratt sought to discredit the very basis of this intervention. His views on the Far East since the war, however, had been strongly individualistic and seem to have been inspired by a passionate concern for the Asian masses and a hatred for those who exploited them. This made him an outspoken advocate of the Chinese Communist revolution although he had no sympathy for the Soviet Union and hoped that China would be spared the evils of Stalinism.[2] Moreover, in his long years in the Consular Service he had developed such a dislike of Americans, and so great an affection for China and the Chinese, that most probably his views and judgements were determined accordingly. Thus, not until the Chinese became involved in the Korean War does he appear to have had any particular theory about its origin, but once they and the Americans were in conflict, it seems there could be no doubt in his own mind where guilt and virtue lay. The present writer, from attending one of the meetings he addressed on the subject, obtained an impression of an impassioned old man, as fully a master of sinister suggestion as his

---

[1] Report of the United Nations Commission on Korea, quoted in the *Survey*, p. 478.

[2] See his article in the *Manchester Guardian*, 14 March 1950, and letter to *The Times*, 11 August 1950. A favourite argument was that the hostile and uncompromising policies of the West, and particularly of the United States, towards revolutionary Asia, were making the triumph of Stalinism more certain.

actor brother, Boris Karloff, and inflamed with an almost personal animosity towards Chiang Kai-shek, MacArthur, Churchill, and British and American governing circles generally.

With regard to the country as a whole, an idea of the size of the minority opposed to intervention in Korea may be gained from the results of a poll taken by the British Institute of Public Opinion on 3 July 1950. In response to the question: 'Do you approve or disapprove of the action that has been taken by the British and American Governments?', 69 per cent registered approval and 14 per cent disapproval. Although too much emphasis should not be placed upon these total figures from an isolated poll, a comparison of the voting figures by parties is none the less significant. Of those who had come to a conclusion, the ratios were: Conservatives—80 per cent approval to 7 per cent disapproval; Labour supporters—63 per cent to 18 per cent; Liberals—72 per cent to 7 per cent.[1] Now it will be noticed that the same proportion of Conservatives and Liberals registered disapproval, namely 7 per cent. In all probability, therefore, this figure was representative of those who objected for reasons unconnected with party beliefs or principles—natural isolationists perhaps, the parents or wives of servicemen, or those for whom war might mean the loss of livelihood. This however still leaves 11 per cent of the Labour supporters opposed to intervention and it is not unreasonable to suppose that these shared the opinions of Davies and Hughes.[2] Tentatively therefore, and bearing in mind the possibility of error when poll percentages are converted into absolute figures, we might, by relating these percentages to the voting strengths of the parties at the General Election of February 1950, conclude that some three and a half millions from all three main

---

[1] For full details of this poll, see Appendix III, D1. The figures given in the *News Chronicle* on 5 July show the Conservative and Liberal votes a little more, the Labour vote a little less favourable to intervention.

[2] That the Parliamentary Labour Party did not contain a similar proportion of dissentients is scarcely surprising, for not only are the extremists, both of Left and Right, more prominent in the constituency parties than in Parliament, but those few Labour M.P.s who had earned themselves the name of 'fellow travellers' had been expelled from the Party the previous year. Moreover, as the Labour Party had an overall majority of only six in the Parliament of 1950–51, there was little disposition among members to rock the boat.

parties were opposed to the action taken by the British and American Governments, and that of these some one and a half millions objected owing to pronounced pacifist or Left-wing sentiments. Taken by themselves these figures are not insignificant, but when set against the total population, they help to bear out the prevailing impression that over Korea the country was pretty well united.

The threat of aggression had brought normally discordant elements to a common resolve. But once the threat had been mastered, it was hardly to be expected that soldiers and politicians, nationalists and internationalists, Right-wingers and radicals, the governments of Pacific powers and those of European, would view the problems posed by the Far Eastern situation in the same light. Nor did they. From the late summer of 1950 controversy over these matters grew.

At the end of September a decision of primary importance had to be taken. The North Koreans—who earlier in the month had looked like expelling the United Nations from their last foothold in the peninsula—were in full retreat before MacArthur's by now superior forces. Should these halt at the Parallel, thus achieving the original aim of repelling aggression, or ought they to follow up their success by advancing deep into North Korea? Although opinion in Britain had, on balance, always favoured caution and restraint in dealing with the revolutionary nationalism of Asia, there was no significant movement against the crossing of the Parallel, and when early in October MacArthur swept on into the North, he did so almost without demur. This, set against the suspicion with which the Left regarded MacArthur, the opposition of Nehru, and the earlier opinion of *The Times* that ' . . . it is not too soon to make plain that the objective is not to conquer the whole of Korea but to drive back the invaders to the line they crossed',[1] may appear surprising. The military situation, however, had so turned in the Allies' favour that to stop at the Parallel seemed madness to some, an impractical rather than a prudent suggestion to others. Nevertheless there was a noticeable difference of view as between Right and Left on how the war should be terminated.

Tory opinion, as revealed in a public opinion poll[2] and the

[1] *The Times*, 5 July 1950.   [2] See Appendix III, D3.

comments of the Conservative press, was much more inclined to favour a military solution, holding that the advance should go on until the North Koreans were finally beaten. That the occupation of North Korea would provoke Russia or China to intervene was not, in the view of the *Daily Telegraph*, to be taken seriously.[1] Such myopic optimism was not general, perhaps not even characteristic, yet it is difficult to resist the conclusion that some sections of Tory opinion—found more amongst the rank and file than the leadership—had the smell of blood in their nostrils and were in no mood to let the quarry go. After the infinite frustration of the cold war, the interminable sterile talks, the feeling of powerlessness in face of a system so ironbound that it seemed to offer no chink which could be prized, there were those for whom the war in Korea came almost as a relief. Here at last was a chance to hit back.

In contrast, Labour and Liberal opinion desired in the main a negotiated settlement.[2] As, however, there were few objections to crossing the Parallel, this meant in effect the offering of generous terms from a position of military advantage. The terms proposed by Bevin, and which largely through his efforts were adopted by the General Assembly, were that Korea should be united, free elections held, and upon the formation of an independent government all forces withdrawn. This solution was even acceptable to the Labour Left, although with the hope not so much that Communism would disappear from the North as that in consequence of the elections the whole country would be enabled to get rid of Rhee and his system. The United Nations Commission, declared the *New Statesman*, should take over the whole of Korea and make sure that the land distribution carried out by the Communists during their brief occupation of the South would be preserved and extended; moreover Peking should be represented on the Commission and as far as possible the settlement should be arranged by Asian countries.[3] Proposals such as these, however, although perhaps admirable in themselves, entirely ignored the realities of the situation. No

[1] *Daily Telegraph*, 30 September 1950.
[2] See Parliamentary and press comment and the public opinion poll of 4 October 1950.
[3] *New Statesman*, 23 September and 7, 14 and 21 October 1950. See also *Tribune*, 6 October 1950.

Communist government ever has submitted or is ever likely to submit its future to the verdict of elections held under non-Communist auspices. Nor was it conceivable that the Americans, who had done most of the fighting, would be willing to leave the peninsula in the hands of a pinkish, neutralist government, even supposing that this is what the Koreans themselves desired. Moreover, any idea that Syngman Rhee would kindly bow himself out, or indeed that he could be got out short of the United Nations' having to fight a second war, this time against the South, was manifestly absurd.

Once the principle of carrying the war into North Korea had been accepted, there was really no alternative but to proceed to the conquest and occupation of the entire country, or halt upon the most militarily defensible line and either bargain from strength or await developments. MacArthur's decision to push on to the Yalu River which formed the frontier with Manchuria, was little criticized in Britain until after the Chinese had intervened. When, however, this occurred and the United Nations forces were thrown back, MacArthur was condemned, particularly on the Left, as a reckless general and, in view of his reported promise to have 'the boys home by Christmas', an irresponsible optimist. He should have stopped, it was widely said, at the narrow 'waist' which bisects North Korea. Were the criticisms justified? That for the most part they were made late rather than early is perhaps significant. For apart from the possibility during October that MacArthur would succeed in his object, there were sound political reasons for advancing to the Yalu. Once the frontier had been secured the United Nations would be free to reconstruct Korea to their liking, the dangers attendant upon the existence in one country of two mutually hostile governments would be removed, and China and Russia would no longer be able to interfere except by themselves engaging in war with the United Nations.

Thus, had MacArthur succeeded, he would doubtless have been hailed as the general who kept his head when all about him were losing theirs. Instead he failed and paid the penalty for failure. Yet his apparent obliviousness to the wider repercussions of his campaign and in particular the probable reactions of China, was rightly deplored. As early as 30 September Chou En-lai announced that his government 'would not stand idly

by when the territory of its neighbour was wantonly invaded'—
a warning also passed on through the Indian ambassador in
Peking.[1] This threat need not necessarily have meant that
intervention would automatically follow a crossing of the
Parallel, for the Communist powers needed to make some protest in view of their allegation that the South had been the
original aggressor. Yet it should have induced wariness. The
British Government was much alive to the danger, advised the
American Government that the advance should be halted at
the waist, and sought both directly and indirectly to reassure
the Chinese.[2] MacArthur in pressing forward was running a
risk, but he was no longer justified in doing so when the risk
became disproportionately great. This it did early in November
when it was discovered that Chinese 'volunteers' were joining
the North Koreans in considerable strength. The seriousness of
this situation led to a number of demands in Britain—particularly one by twenty-two Labour M.P.s—that the Government
should seek agreement on a line beyond which the United
Nations forces would not go.[3] The Government did in fact
urge this course upon the Americans,[4] but on 26 November
MacArthur launched his much publicized final offensive which
was to bring the war to a speedy close. Almost immediately it
was thrown back by an attack of 200,000 Chinese.

One piece of retrospective criticism concerning this first
phase of the Korean War might be looked at. In his *History of
the Cold War*, published in 1955, Kenneth Ingram, a writer of
liberal outlook, one prepared to believe that Communist actions
and attitudes were sometimes born of justifiable apprehension,

[1] See: *Survey of International Affairs, 1949–50*, p. 351; K. M. Pannikar, *In
Two Chinas*, p. 110.

[2] See: Bevin, H.C. Debs. Vol. 482. Cols. 1459–61 (14 December 1950);
K. Younger, *Socialist Foreign Policy* (Fabian International Bureau, Tract
287), April 1951, p. 25. The British Chiefs of Staff advised consolidation at
the Korean waist. The British *Chargé* at Peking was instructed to inform the
Chinese Government that there would be no attack upon Manchuria. An
American writer, Allen S. Whiting, *China Crosses the Yalu*, has claimed that
the Chinese Communists intervened only after much hesitation and that
had the North Korean régime been assured of some territorial basis, even a
limited one, would probably not have done so.

[3] The creation of a buffer zone was also advocated by *The Times, Manchester Guardian, Economist, Daily Herald* and *New Statesman*.

[4] Attlee, H.C. Debs, Vol. 481. Col. 1437 (30 November 1950).

maintained that in allowing their forces to cross the Parallel, the United Nations were guilty 'not merely of an error of strategy but of an infringement of a vital principle'.

They were acting no longer as police, but as co-belligerents on the side of the South Koreans. They should have halted their forces, guarded South Korea against further invasion, and called upon both the North and South Koreans to appear in the court of the United Nations and present their case, warning the North Koreans that if they failed to appear, judgement would be pronounced in their absence.[1]

It is not difficult to imagine what would have happened had this course been adopted. The North Koreans, while continuing to denounce the United Nations' action as an American conspiracy, would have utilized the inevitable delay to recover their military balance, fortify their frontier, and perhaps invite in the Chinese in overwhelming strength. Thus for the Allies to have halted at the Parallel would in practice have been foolish, but what of the issue of principle? In maintaining that the United Nations had acted illegally, Ingram employed this analogy:

If one of the litigants in a civil suit takes the law into his own hands, enters the house of his opponent and assaults him, the task of the police is to eject him, and to place him under restraint until the case is brought to court. They would be acting wrongfully if they punished the offender before the court had delivered judgment, if for example they broke into his house and proceeded to break up his furniture.

The obvious answer to this is that the United Nations invasion of the North was never conceived as some old-time punitive expedition in which the pursuing army laid waste the native villages before returning to base. The intention was to arrange a permanent settlement so that the trouble would not recur. In order to do this it was first necessary to break the North Korean power to resist, just as the first task of the police must be to disarm whomever they apprehend. MacArthur had given the North Koreans an opportunity of laying down their arms before he crossed the Parallel, but his summons was ignored. Moreover, the North Koreans had surely forfeited all right to

[1] Kenneth Ingram, op. cit., p. 224.

the protection of their frontier and to a United Nations inquiry when they ignored the original call of the Security Council to withdraw from South Korean territory.

Thus the breach of principle argument would appear to be untenable—or at least quixotic—and this probably explains the slight degree of support it received at the time. In Parliament the Left-wing Labour M.P. Sydney Silverman alone seems to have propounded it, although Lord Chorley came near to doing so when he declared that in invading North Korea the West had shown lack of moral strength.[1] The *Manchester Guardian* did indeed talk of 'converting' the non-infringement of the Parallel into a point of principle, but then proceeded to give reasons why to cross would be inexpedient.[2]

The respective demands of principle and expediency are a perpetual trouble to the liberal or radical. In his deep feeling for the common people living under systems alien and often hostile to his own, in his desire to encourage respect for the rule of law, and in his anxiety to prove himself a fair-minded internationalist not indifferent to, but not to be swayed by, the interests of his country, he is watchful, in small matters as in great, that his own government does not depart from the high standards which he expects of it. But at once a difficulty arises. For in an ideologically riven world in which realism has to confront realism if equilibrium is to be maintained, not only is the liberal or radical idealist an uncharacteristic figure, but his standards, if scrupulously adhered to, could well lead to disaster. As E. H. Carr has shown in *The Twenty Years' Crisis*, a plethora of idealism was in large part responsible for the calamitous happenings of the 1930s. Since the war, however, the great majority of liberals and radicals have been content to compromise and nowhere is this better shown than during the opening phase in Korea. Some remained uneasy over the fact that the Security Council took its decisions in the absence of one —or without quibbling, two—of its permanent members, and most continued to press hard for Communist China's admission. Again, they were flatly opposed to any attempt by Syngman Rhee to extend his rule into North Korea in the wake of Mac-

[1] Silverman, H.C. Debs. Vol. 481. Cols. 1275-6 (29 November 1950); Lord Chorley, H.L. Debs. Vol. 169. Col. 319 (15 November 1950).
[2] *Manchester Guardian*, 30 September 1950.

Arthur's advance. Yet they supported what was in effect an American rather than a truly international undertaking, and in the main they concurred in the decision to put an end to a régime guilty of aggression. For as all but a few, chiefly of the older generation, had come to realize, in practice there was no choice.

VI

The Korean War: *China Intervenes*

The intervention of China in the Korean War brought the Far Eastern crisis to its flash-point and for some months it was doubtful whether a much greater war than that raging in the Korean peninsula could be prevented. All really turned upon the conflict of forces, interests, personalities, emotions and arguments within the United States. For, with China, through lack of sea and air power, obliged to confine her operations to Korea, the United States alone—unless, improbably, the Soviet Union chose to take the offensive—was capable of turning a minor war into a major. In this conflict between bellicosity and restraint, the attitude of Great Britain, although it may not have been a deciding, was certainly a contributory factor in the determination of the outcome. At the diplomatic level the British Government, in close and constant touch with the American, used all its influence against any policy or proposal likely to produce a general war with China. In this it reflected prevailing opinion in Britain, which had, however, an additional importance. For one thing, comment as expressed in Parliament or the press might be usefully outspoken when the Government, for obvious reasons, had to be silent or circumspect. For another, it was possible to publicize opinions in Britain which, owing to the McCarthy hysteria, could not be effectively expressed in the United States even though they might be generally subscribed to by the mass of the American people. Thus, to judge by the noise they made and the coverage they were given, the China Lobbyists might be thought to have had a popular backing, yet upon the supreme issue of whether or not the war should be extended to China, a public opinion survey of February 1951 reveals that the American public was as overwhelmingly against such a course as was the British.[1] Moreover, although over some matters British opinion was sharply divided from American,

[1] See Appendix III, D10 note.

H

many American liberals seem to have held that upon the whole this transatlantic influence was salutary.

The main difference between the American attitude and the British over the intervention of Communist China in Korea, was that whereas the Americans regarded war with China, even though hostilities might be confined to the peninsula, as having begun, the British did not. This was reflected in a number of Anglo–American disagreements and misunderstandings, especially during the winter of 1950–1. To the British, the American partiality for strong counter-measures seemed like recklessness; to the Americans, the British desire to preserve their tenuous diplomatic and rather more than tenuous commercial relationship with Communist China appeared to betoken either softness or perfidy.

At the end of November 1950, the strength of British feeling over a possible enlargement or intensification of the war was swiftly and strikingly manifested. For several weeks the news from Korea had been received with increasing disquietude. The wisdom of MacArthur's final offensive, launched as it was in the face of mounting Chinese opposition, seemed to many to be doubtful in the extreme. After the Chinese counter-offensive, demands from MacArthur's supporters in Congress that Manchuria should be bombed caused fresh alarm. But it was a report that the President himself was contemplating the use of the atomic bomb in North Korea which brought matters to a head. In Parliament the news created a sensation.[1] 'Not in the darkest days of the war', said one observer, 'was the House so disturbed as it was over Mr. Truman's statement to his press conference on the atomic bomb.'[2] Silverman immediately got over a hundred of his colleagues to sign a letter to the Prime Minister urging the withdrawal of British troops from Korea if the bomb should be dropped. This was no usual Left-wing back-bench demonstration, but the protest of fully one-third of the Parliamentary Labour Party including several members of the national executive. Nor was the concern of the Opposition any the less; indeed there was some criticism from the Conservative benches that the Government had not pressed its views forcefully enough upon the Americans. That he should

[1] See H.C. Debs. Vol. 481. Cols. 1382–1440 (30 November 1950).
[2] Westminster correspondent of the *Spectator*, 8 December 1950.

immediately fly to Washington was urged upon Attlee from all quarters of the House, and although a later and more complete report of Truman's statement revealed that the worst fears had been unfounded, the need for consultation and reassurance in the light of the latest events was obvious.

Attlee's visit to Truman early in December 1950 was after-wards made much of by his own supporters. Indeed, some Left-wing speakers and broadcasters gave the impression that by his dramatic intervention the Labour leader had somehow staved off a Third World War. Although this was good election stuff, the truth was more prosaic. The President and his advisers were no more keen on a general war with China than were the British, and both sides agreed on the necessity of fighting it out in Korea. Over Formosa and the Chinese seat—which the British, but not the Americans, were willing to include in a general settlement—there was no agreement. As for the atomic bomb, the subject was merely raised by Attlee in an informal way at the end of the talks. Truman reassured him that there was no danger of its immediate use and undertook to inform the British Government of any developments which might bring about a change of mind.[1] The Prime Minister had done as well as could be expected, and this was generally realized. Such differences as existed were inevitable, for they largely arose out of the British Government's dread of alienating Asian opinion, and the American Government's concern not to do anything that would clearly be repugnant to the majority of its people.

Although these talks had done much to clear the air, opinion in Britain continued in a state of excitement and apprehension. There was a difference, however, in the reactions of Right and Left. Both were gravely concerned at the possibility of the United States becoming involved in a general war with China, but Tory opinion was chiefly preoccupied with the bad effect that this would have upon Anglo–American relations and the defence of Europe. Since the intervention in Tibet and Korea and following the uncompromising and bitter attacks of General Wu upon the Western powers during his appearance before the United Nations in November, few Tories believed that there was anything to be gained from placating the Chinese, or that

[1] For a full account of the talks see: Harry S. Truman, *Years of Trial and Hope 1946–1953*, Chapter XXV.

to give way over the Chinese seat and Formosa while the Communists were advancing in Korea was other than the height of foolishness.

Radical opinion, on the other hand, still considered that it was imperative to meet Peking half way, in the interests both of a settlement and of retaining Asian goodwill. This point of view had been put to Truman by Attlee. Yet whereas the Government was not outwardly critical of American policy and saw the best hope for moderation in maintaining a close and understanding relationship between itself and the American Administration, there tended to arise on the Left at this time a movement that was as strongly and as outspokenly against war with China as a section of American opinion was for it. In a spirited correspondence to the press, in increased activity by the forty years old National Peace Council, in meetings and demonstrations, and, most significantly, in the formation of a new body called the Peace with China Council, the movement of protest gathered force.[1] Such developments were not confined to London, nor yet to the Left. The response from the provinces was swift and impressive, and intellectuals of varying political views lent their support. Communists and fellow-travellers naturally cashed in, but in the main the peace movement was the spontaneous reaction of those who considered that the West stood in danger of being tempted or led into a course that was as futile and perilous as it was reactionary and wicked.

Early in 1951 a circumstance arose which brought out clearly the differences between the Tory and Left-wing attitudes. The intervention of the Chinese Communists and the defeats they were inflicting upon MacArthur's army had a profound effect upon American opinion. Peking had clearly committed aggression in the view of most Americans, and the Administration came under strong pressure to take some effective counter-action. The American Government's own reaction was to lay before the Political Committee of the General Assembly a resolution seeking to condemn China as an aggressor and to invite the consideration of further measures against her.

In general, Tory opinion was not unsympathetic to this proposal. During the first days of January the Chinese had not only advanced beyond the Parallel and captured Seoul, the Southern

[1] See Appendix II.

capital, but had rebuffed American efforts to obtain a cease-fire. In the words of the *Daily Telegraph* (19 January):

In these circumstances there would seem to be no choice but to proceed to the next logical step, which is to declare Communist China an aggressor. Merely, however, to pass a resolution to that effect . . . is no more than a gesture, worthless, and even harmful, unless it results in effective action.

Moreover, as those who supported the American resolution argued, to denounce a small power for aggression but not a large one would savour of moral cowardice. But these were subsidiary considerations; as before, the heart of the Tory case was the overriding importance of running in harness with the Americans—particularly at a time of grave crisis and in approaching an issue about which the American Government and people were determined and united.[1]

In contrast, many liberals and radicals and the whole of the 'peace with China' school were seriously alarmed. They believed that, with patience, a truce could still be negotiated, but that the branding of China as an aggressor would make it almost impossible to achieve. They believed too, that if, as seemed likely, such a move was to be followed by a blockade, a general war with China would almost certainly ensue. Apart from these practical objections, it was held doubtful whether China had in fact committed aggression and that to class her with North Korea was absurd. As one Labour M.P. put it in answer to an Opposition member's charge of appeasement:

When Germany was appeased by the Tory pre-war Government, she was a naked and unprovoked aggressor, whereas the whole essence of the issue in regard to China is that, unfortunately, by the saddest development of events and as the result of an advance made contrary to the advice of the British Cabinet and the British Chiefs of Staff, the whole matter developed in a way which many of us on this side of the House . . . believe rendered China's intervention understandable. . . . China, as she saw her territory approached by the forces mainly of a Great Power which had not recognized her Government, led by a commander whose association with the Chinese Nationalists and Chiang Kai-shek was extremely well-

[1] See Churchill, H.C. Debs. Vol. 483. Cols. 42 (23 January) and 1084-5 (1 February 1951).

known could reasonably and understandably regard her security as threatened.[1]

This was a favourite argument of the critics of American policy. Manchuria being the Chinese Ruhr and its industry largely dependent upon the Yalu power-stations, Peking, they declared, was fully justified in regarding MacArthur's final advance as a threat to her national security and in taking the necessary counter-measures. When such measures involved the reoccupation of North Korea and an attempted reconquest of the South, their defensive nature might be called in question, but there was a disposition to give Peking the benefit of the doubt. After all, had not the United Nations attempted, in reverse, the very same thing, and with the best of intentions?

How far the Government was influenced by this approach to the matter is difficult to determine, but the diplomatic correspondent of the *Manchester Guardian* reported on 24 January that the cabinet was split over the American resolution. In view of the fact that two of its more Leftward looking members, Bevan and Wilson, were becoming increasingly restive prior to their resignations in April, this is indeed likely, but in the end the Government agreed to a compromise. It reluctantly supported the resolution declaring Communist China an aggressor, but refused to accept the clauses referring to Peking's rejection of all peace proposals. Moreover, it insisted that a Good Offices Committee should further explore the possibilities of a peaceful solution before a report was made on the possible employment of sanctions.[2] There was much to be said for this course. Had Britain opposed the resolution outright, not only would it have been passed in its original and more stringent form, but the spirit of mutual confidence and accommodation which had grown up between the two governments might well have been endangered. The amended resolution was adopted by the General Assembly on 1 February 1951.

The Government's handling of this matter won Tory approval, but was far from pleasing to the Labour Left and the 'peace with China' group. For even though the Government had got the Americans to accept the milder version, and not

---

[1] A. J. Irvine, H.C. Debs. Vol. 484. Cols. 481–2 (14 February 1951).
[2] See G. L. Goodwin, *Britain and the United Nations*, pp. 138–40.

without a struggle, Britain had nevertheless supported a step which they regarded as both momentous and tragic. An article in the *New Statesman* headed 'China Branded'—the term the critics usually employed—described the resolution as being one more milestone on the road to World War III. On the same day (3 February) letters to *The Times* from leading members both of the Left wing of the Parliamentary Labour Party and also of the Peace with China Council, dwelt on the seriousness of the situation now that the resolution had been adopted.

Such forebodings are in part to be explained by the sanguine view of Communism, and particularly of Chinese Communism, still entertained in radical and Left-wing circles. China's condemnation, it was held, would be fatal to a peaceful settlement. Had not the Chinese themselves so informed the Indian ambassador? But that a Communist government, whose spokesmen and propagandists habitually referred to the United Nations action in Korea in terms of unparalleled abuse, would be seriously affected by the passing of a declaration from which no immediate action was to ensue, was scarcely credible. To hold otherwise was to reveal oneself ignorant of Marxist method and purpose. If the Chinese leaders had concluded that there was nothing further to be gained from military action, it is difficult to believe that a mere declaration of this sort would have prevented the negotiation of a truce. On the other hand, if they were prepared to let the fighting continue, they would be likely, for the sake of the effect upon Asian opinion, to claim that the Western declaration alone was the obstacle to peace. That it was such an obstacle, inasmuch as the Chinese might have considered the propaganda advantage it gave them to be worth the cost of more fighting, is indeed just possible, but in view of the heavy demands the war would make upon an economy needing to be reorganized and developed, highly unlikely.

There was, however, a more valid objection: the declaration, although relatively innocuous in itself, might well provide the thin end of the wedge for the militarists and the China Lobby. For Peking having been formally proclaimed an aggressor, the demand for sanctions and reprisals could not, it was held, be indefinitely deferred. Moreover, in subscribing to the resolution, had not Britain put herself in a weak position for resisting further measures? Few, even of the Left, would have gone so far as G. D. H. Cole who wanted Britain to lead a 'Third Force' and who declared that in the event of war between China and the Western powers he would be on the side of China,[1] yet apprehension over future American policy was at this time widespread. That this was so was largely owing to a great and growing distrust of General MacArthur.

For an American military leader, MacArthur emerged from the war with a reputation in Britain probably second only to Eisenhower's.[2] Although little was known of him as a man, he was personally identified, as no other commander, with a great campaign from initial disaster to ultimate triumph. Mac-Arthur's military renown persisted, but as master of post-war Japan he was more doubtfully regarded. Few denied that his achievement in turning the country into something like a modern Western democratic state had been a remarkable one, but his autocratic rule, his aloofness, and his virtual disregard of the representatives of those allied powers for which also he acted as Supreme Commander, caused resentment. In the words of the *Economist* (14 April 1951):

He had a manner of speech and an air which frightened Europeans, who have had their full measure of strong and headstrong men in the last twenty years. He became a symbol of the American self-confidence, impatience for results and enjoyment of power which reveal themselves more conspicuously outside than inside the United States. . . . Indeed it has to be said quite frankly that in many countries—certainly in Britain—General MacArthur had become the focus of anti-American feeling.

This hostility was most marked on the Left. To some extent it owed itself to his being a Right-wing Republican and closely linked with certain of the more reactionary elements in American public life. Some critics recalled that when Chief of Staff at Washington during the Slump, he had somewhat brutally broken up an army of unemployed encamped before the White House. But more immediate misgivings were aroused by his attitude towards Asia and the Asians. His message of 24 August

---

[1] Article in the *New Statesman*, 3 February 1951.

[2] In Lord Alanbrooke's estimation he was the greatest general and best strategist that the war produced, see Arthur Bryant, *Triumph in the West*, p. 513.

1950 to the veterans' convention, in which he declared that he knew the Oriental mind, that it admired 'aggressive, resolute and dynamic leadership', and that 'nothing could be more fallacious than the threadbare argument . . . that if we defend Formosa we alienate continental Asia', achieved a certain notoriety in Britain as elsewhere.

After the Chinese intervention, British opinion became increasingly disturbed by MacArthur's ideas as to how the situation could best be met. His proposals that Chinese airbases in Manchuria should be attacked, that hostile aircraft should be pursued across the Yalu, and that the Nationalists should be allowed to raid the mainland in order to relieve pressure in Korea, were all condemned as being likely to provoke a general war. The British Government was naturally opposed to these suggestions. With regard to the bombing of Manchuria it had an agreement with the Americans that no action was to be taken without prior consultation, and Truman found it useful to remind MacArthur of this.[1] On the question of the Nationalist raids, it took the strongest possible exception, asking for an Embassy inquiry, to MacArthur's letter of 20 March 1951 to Joseph Martin, the Republican Congressional leader, in which he advocated these.[2]

In the main, Tory opinion was much less critical of MacArthur during the autumn and winter of 1950–51 than Liberal and Labour opinion.[3] Indeed, leading Conservatives often spoke bitterly of those who attacked him.[4] They naturally felt that such criticisms were damaging Anglo–American relations. To some extent, however, theirs seems also to have been an instinctive reaction, just as it was in the days of Haig, Robertson and the Liberal ministers of the First World War—the eagerness of the military party to protect a serving soldier from critical and interfering civilians who were not on the spot and were assumed to know little or nothing of war and military affairs.

---

[1] Harry S. Truman, *Years of Trial and Hope 1946–1953*, pp. 396–7.

[2] See: the *Observer*, 8 April 1951, a speech at Cardiff by Kenneth Younger, Minister of State; ibid., a report by the diplomatic correspondent.

[3] For public opinion, see Appendix III, D 7.

[4] E.g. Conservative anger at a speech by Woodrow Wyatt, H.C. Debs. Vol. 478. Cols. 1341–47 (14 September 1950); Lord Salisbury on a speech by Shinwell, H.L. Debs. Vol. 169. Cols. 989–90 (14 December 1950).

Early in the spring of 1951 MacArthur began openly to challenge Truman's policy, a course which if suffered to continue, would have undermined the President's authority. In consequence, British Tories were hard put to defend him against Labour and Liberal critics who now claimed that in this they were for the President—and most gave up trying. During late March and early April criticism of MacArthur swiftly mounted, and relief at his dismissal on 11 April was general. All the national papers except the *Daily Express* welcomed the news, and in the House of Commons it was greeted with cheers. A poll taken a month later revealed that Conservatives approved of Truman's action by 2 to 1, Labour supporters and Liberals by nearly 5 to 1.[1]

Leaving aside his final, indefensible behaviour, to what extent were the attacks upon MacArthur justified? Were his proposals, in fact, as irresponsible and reckless as his British critics usually made them out to be? One factor at least seems to have been given insufficient attention in Britain: the military. On 26 August 1950 Churchill had complained in a broadcast of the tardiness of the Government in despatching troops to Korea. Two battalions only arrived for the defence of Pusan, and the eventual British contingent was never more than a small fraction of the American. The total United States casualties for the whole war amounted to over 140,000, more than half of these being incurred during the first twelve months. The equivalent British figure was under 4,500. Churchill often drew attention to the extent of the American contribution, and to the sacrifice it entailed; but it does not seem to have made much impression upon British opinion, and there was certainly no widespread feeling that in Korea Britain should have done much more than she did. Many indeed felt that the country had enough on its hands in Malaya and that this was insufficiently appreciated in America, but in all probability there was a deeper reason: a nation which had lost 60,000 during a single day's fighting on the Somme, and had alone fought both world wars from start to finish, might well consider that it had already had more than its share of blood-letting. Nevertheless, there might have been a better appreciation of MacArthur's difficulties. Twice he was hard pressed and thus he had a good excuse—certainly a

[1] See Appendix III, D9.

better one than was often allowed—for seeking ways of relieving the pressure and conserving the lives of his men.

But was this his object?—or did he intend, as many of his British critics firmly believed, to launch a major war upon Communism? The course which MacArthur favoured after the Chinese intervention has been described by Truman:

This provided for a blockade by the United Nations of the coast of China and called for the bombing of the Chinese mainland. Mac-Arthur also specified that the maximum use be made of Chinese Nationalist forces in Korea, and at the same time troops of Chiang Kai-shek would be 'introduced' into South China, possibly through Hong Kong.[1]

MacArthur himself averred that these measures were simply to be employed to restore the situation in Korea, but Truman's comment is illuminating:

I have never been able to make myself believe that MacArthur, seasoned soldier that he was, did not realize that the 'introduction of Chinese Nationalist forces into South China' would be an act of war; or that he, who had had a front-row seat at world events for thirty-five years, did not realize that the Chinese people would react to the bombing of their cities in exactly the same manner as the people of the United States reacted to the bombing of Pearl Harbor; or that, with his knowledge of the East, he could have overlooked the fact that after he had bombed the cities of China there would still be vast flows of materials from Russia so that, if he wanted to be con-sistent, his next step would have to be the bombardment of Vladi-vostok and of the Trans-Siberian railroad! But because I was sure that MacArthur could not possibly have overlooked these considera-tions, I was left with just one simple conclusion: General MacArthur was ready to risk general war. I was not.[2]

In Britain, the view that the West should be ready to risk a general war over Korea found at least one advocate in intellec-tual circles. Writing in the January edition (1951) of the

[1] Harry S. Truman, *Years of Trial and Hope 1946–1953*, p. 440.

[2] Ibid., pp. 440–1. In a memorandum he submitted to Eisenhower, then President elect, on 17 December 1952, MacArthur advocated—in the event of Stalin's not agreeing to American proposals for a Korean and general world settlement—the atomic bombing of North Korea and liberation of China by the Nationalists with American support. See: Douglas MacArthur, *Reminiscences*, pp. 410–1.

Twentieth Century, G. F. Hudson, in an article headed 'Privileged Sanctuary', described the situation as it had existed since the Chinese intervention, as 'unprecedented' and 'absurd'. Whereas others regarded the policy of limited war as prudent, he denounced it as cowardly, and the reasons given for it as hypocritical:

It will probably be some time before the British public realizes just what has happened or the extent of the political defeat which has been incurred. For defeat it is, whatever the euphemisms employed to conceal it, and it is a defeat far more in will and purpose than in the actual contest of arms. The British may deceive themselves with talk about 'calm', 'statesmanship' and preference for a 'political solution', but all Asia can see that America, Britain and the majority of the United Nations, after carrying on warfare for five months against North Korea, have flinched from a challenge to war when it was issued by China. The warrior who, after overcoming a weak adversary seeks to evade battle against a stronger antagonist cannot convincingly claim that love of peace or moral scruples against the use of force inspire his action. . . . In the eyes of everyone who has not an interest in covering his disgrace, he has run away from the challenge, and his reputation suffers accordingly.

Hudson then made the point that if the Allies had resolved beforehand not to fight it out with China and Russia if those two powers had intervened, then their invasion of North Korea was a 'reckless gamble'. Alternatively, if the Allied leaders had not considered what to do until Chinese troops had actually entered Korea, they had proved themselves thoughtless and negligent—a charge levelled against the British Government in particular.

With regard to what should have been or ought to be done, Hudson was less explicit, but he would have 'expected' the Allies to warn Peking that unless Chinese troops were withdrawn from Korea within a set time, Manchuria would be bombed. Had this been done, he declared, either the Chinese would have been evacuated, or Chinese industry and communications in Manchuria would have been destroyed, or Russia would have intervened with world war as the probable result.

It was certainly true that the advance into North Korea was undertaken without much regard to the possible repercussions, but in directing his censures chiefly at the British Government,

Hudson showed bias. He said nothing, for example, about the British proposal to halt at and hold the 'waist', nor did he place the blame for the Yalu fiasco where it chiefly lay. Indeed, the impression given is that the British, pitiably addicted to appeasement and the wishful thinking of the Left, and unable to take other than a 'parochial' (i.e. Europe first) view of the East–West conflict, had dissuaded the American leaders against their better judgement from executing sound, realistic measures. Yet it was just such a policy as Hudson apparently favoured that Truman and his advisers regarded as too risky to be attempted. And if the invasion of North Korea had been a 'reckless gamble', what, it may be asked, would have been the taking of a step which Hudson himself considered might well lead to world war? Admittedly the bombing of Manchuria was later, even by the Labour Government, contemplated as a possible measure, but this was to deter the Chinese from taking additional action, not to force them to abandon a course already begun. That they would have done so had such a threat been pressed is inconceivable, for practically no ultimatum has had its intended effect upon a great power, let alone a revolutionary one for whom 'face' is a prime consideration. The result would therefore have been to extend the war to Manchuria, and then, if the logic of the argument was to be maintained, to other 'privileged sanctuaries' beyond. Nor should it be forgotten, that if Manchuria was a privileged sanctuary, so too was Japan.

Elsewhere in his writings, Hudson's criticisms of Anglo-Saxon wishful thinking and naïve idealism have bite and point, but in equating a policy of belligerent recklessness with the traditional realism he believed himself to be advocating, this legatee of the Enlightenment[1] showed himself for once to be less than enlightened. We have already noted his view that Hellas should be more aware of and better prepared against the growing threat of resurgent barbarism, but to advocate risking a major and perhaps world conflict as though it were but a latter-day Battle of Marathon, might cause it to be wondered where the greatest threat to Hellas really lay.

[1] See Hudson's article, 'Toynbee versus Gibbon', *Twentieth Century*, November 1954, p. 412.

VII

The Korean War: *Stalemate and Truce*

Shortly after the dismissal of MacArthur, the Korean War entered its third, final, and longest phase. By June the war of movement was over, and so was much of the uncertainty. MacArthur's successors were younger, purely professional men, unlikely to disobey the directives given them or to take important political or strategical decisions without reference to Washington. At this point much of the real tension disappeared, although there were moments during the further two years that the war was to last when British apprehensions were revived and Anglo–American frictions renewed.

At the time of MacArthur's recall, however, the future course of the war was still very much an open question. Ever since the second Communist invasion of South Korea had been stayed and reversed in February 1951, Western attention had been engaged by the problem of what the United Nations were to do now that they had regained the initiative. The prevailing opinion in Britain was that there should be no further attempt to occupy North Korea, but that the advance should be halted in the region of the Parallel so that peace might the more easily be negotiated. There was no marked difference between Left and Right over this, and the same view was shared by the Government.[1]

Partly this was a reaction against MacArthur. If he were again permitted to invade North Korea, might he not make another bid for the Yalu, or at least try to enlarge the war? But even after he had gone, there was little enthusiasm for a drive to the North. Now that China had intervened, and the conquest of the whole country had been made virtually impracticable, there was a widespread feeling, not only in Britain, but, with

---

[1] See: Attlee, H.C. Debs. Vol. 484. Cols. 61–3 (12 February 1951); Shinwell, ibid. Vol. 485. Col. 2434 (21 March); debate on the matter, ibid. Cols. 2673–82 (22 March). Public opinion is indicated by the poll taken on 20 February, see Appendix III, D8.

the exception of South Korea, throughout the United Nations alliance, that the war should be brought to a close as rapidly as possible. It remains to ask, however, whether halting the advance in the neighbourhood of the Parallel was the best way to achieve results—or whether those who advocated such a course were not as naïvely optimistic in one direction as the MacArthur school were dangerous and rash in the other.

The policy, when tried, at first produced encouraging results. On 23 June 1951, after both Trygve Lie and Acheson had declared that a cease fire approximately along the Parallel would fulfil the Organization's purpose of repelling aggression, Jacob Malik, the Soviet representative to the Security Council, announced that in the Russian government's view truce talks should be held. The Chinese welcomed this move—which they themselves had probably suggested—and the first meeting took place at Kaesong on 10 July.

The expected peace, however, did not transpire. The talks dragged on for over two years largely because neither side was willing to give way over the repatriation of prisoners of war.[1] Although no strategical offensive was undertaken during this period, the fighting was far from being nominal, the Americans alone suffering a further 65,000 casualties in the course of it. Moreover, the Communists, who were at some disadvantage militarily when the truce talks began, used the time gained so to strengthen their position that it could thereafter be forced only at immense cost.

In view of this it might seem that it was foolish not to have advanced to the Korean waist when the opportunity allowed, for occupation of a large area of North Korean territory would have placed the United Nations in a far better bargaining position for bringing the war to an early close. However, the prevailing view that peace should be negotiated on a basis of equality rather than of superiority was probably a sound one. Had the advance continued to the waist, the Communists might

---

[1] Large numbers of North Korean and Chinese prisoners refused repatriation and the United Nations declared that no prisoner should be sent back against his will. The Communists on their part insisted that all prisoners should be returned, arguing that this was demanded by the Geneva Convention. For a discussion of the prisoner question and the legal implications of the Geneva Convention, see Guy Wint, *What Happened in Korea?*, Chapter XV, pp. 72–83.

not even have been willing to negotiate; on the contrary the Chinese might well have drawn further upon their immense reserves of manpower to throw the allies back once more beyond the Parallel. Admittedly this is conjectural, but it should be borne in mind that the Korean War, even though on a limited scale, was the first trial of military strength between Communism and Western democracy, that it was fought out in a part of the world where each had much to gain or lose, and that in consequence prestige was more than usually important. Neither side, therefore, once the great powers were engaged, could be expected to acquiesce in the other's occupying the whole or major portion of a disputed territory if it could muster sufficient strength to prevent it. In such case the conflict would end only when both sides stood to lose the minimum of prestige.

On a more philosophical level, seeing that every war compels an acceptance of reality, it may be doubted whether the Korean conflict could end otherwise than as a stalemate. For unlike in a general war in which the total strength of the contestants is engaged, the reality in this case lay outside the war, in the equilibrium in which the Western and Communist worlds stood to each other. Thus, until and unless the fighting in Korea could become very much more than marginal, the East–West equilibrium might be expected to re-establish itself there as elsewhere. And so it turned out. Every advance beyond the Parallel provoked an effective reaction, so that like a bow-string returning to the mean of least tension, the fighting line in Korea reverted by diminishing oscillations to the region in which it had begun.

Whether or not the stabilization of the front in the vicinity of the Parallel was the prerequisite for an eventual truce, it meant that the opportunities for putting pressure upon the Chinese were now confined to trade embargoes and the heavier damage and casualties that could be inflicted mainly by superior airpower. The question of how far, if at all, pressure should be exerted by these means, gave rise to controversy and comment during the remainder of the war, and led to further Anglo–American frictions.

The basic difference of view between the British and the Americans as to whether or not they were at war with China, was reflected in the embargo controversy during the spring of

1951. Criticism, particularly after the fall of MacArthur, mounted in the United States over Britain's China trade. To most Americans it seemed monstrous that at the same time as American troops were being killed by Chinese shells and bullets, the British should persist in supplying China with goods. Moreover, it was not simply a rumour or an unsubstantiated accusation of McCarthy's that some of the commodities had a military value, for General MacArthur himself had claimed at the Senate hearings which followed his recall that strategic materials were reaching the Chinese through Hong Kong.

The bad effect upon American opinion gravely concerned the Opposition, various members of which had for some months been questioning the Government on the China trade. When the subject was debated on 7 and 10 May 1951, Churchill was for stopping altogether the Malayan rubber shipments in order to help restore Anglo–American harmony.[1] Labour opinion, on the other hand, in general welcomed this commercial inter-course, believing that it would smooth the way to a settlement in Korea. Indeed, for the Left it was the material counterpart of recognition; it had the merit of meeting Asian nationalism half-way. To abandon it would not only cause trouble through-out Asia, but also, it was held, be a step nearer to the disastrous policy of blockade. In any case the effect would be to integrate the Chinese and Russian economies. As for American criti-cisms of the trade Britain allowed between her Asian colonies and China, Labour members were quick to point out that MacArthur himself had permitted Japan to increase her exports to Communist China during 1950—a counter-charge deplored by Churchill on the grounds that the Americans were bearing a far greater burden.[2]

The Government reacted sharply to the more irresponsible allegations and sought also to make its own case clear. On 7 May 1951, Sir Hartley Shawcross, the President of the Board of Trade, declared that since the start of the Korean War, the sending of goods of direct military importance to China had been totally prohibited.[3] Three days later he dealt with Mac-Arthur's charges. The General, he said, had quoted from a list

---

[1] H.C. Debs. Vol. 487. Cols. 1598, 2166, 2170.
[2] Ibid. Cols. 1594 (7 May); 2166, 2186–7, 2201–4 (10 May 1951). See also the *New Statesman*, leading article, 12 May.   [3] Ibid. Col. 1589.

of exports to China which the Hong Kong Government had voluntarily and periodically sent to the Supreme Commander. Some of the materials cited were certainly strategic, but, Shawcross added, MacArthur had neglected to mention that against these were *nil* returns! He had, moreover, quoted things which were not of strategic importance, and had also included cameras in his list even though only one was sent. Britain, in fact, had been more restrictive in this matter than anyone apart from the United States, but the Government did not impose a total embargo as the Americans had done, and for three reasons. First, Britain had often to get essential supplies from Communist countries; second, in the Government's view the stopping of all trade would prejudice the chances of a Korean settlement; third, it would also affect the economies of Britain's Far Eastern colonies, and in particular bring hardship to Hong Kong. With regard to the last point, a similar consideration, Shawcross observed, had no doubt led MacArthur to permit Japanese exports to Communist China to rise from a monthly average of half a million dollars during the first half of 1950, to one of three and a half million during its final quarter.[1]

The Truman Administration had shown understanding of the British position, but its opponents had clearly chosen to exploit the matter of Britain's China trade for their own purposes, and this had had its effect upon American public opinion. In order to correct these impressions, Sir Oliver Franks, the British ambassador, made a nation-wide broadcast to the American people on 18 May. Defending British policy, he repeated the arguments quoted above and also referred to MacArthur's allowing Japanese exports to China to increase 'very considerably' during 1950.[2] Until then few had known about this in the United States. The ambassador's broadcast was generally praised in the British press, the only complaint being that the Americans should have been told such things much earlier.

In respect of Malaya's rubber exports, however, criticism of the Government was surely justified. During the latter half of 1950, 70,700 tons of rubber reached China from British Far Eastern territories—chiefly Malaya—compared with only

---

[1] Ibid. Cols. 2185–86 (10 May 1951).
[2] *The Times, Daily Telegraph*, etc., 19 May 1951.

15,881 tons during the latter half of 1949.[1] By March 1951 the amount of Malayan rubber sent to China since the beginning of the Korean War had reached 120,000 tons—almost three times as much as had gone to the U.S.S.R. over the same period.[2] When the importance of rubber in modern warfare is considered, the supplying of China with 100,000 tons more than her estimated civilian requirements during those critical months, must be regarded, despite the difficulty of controlling the exports by licensing, as a highly irresponsible proceeding.[3]

In April 1951, the Government decided to limit the exports of Malayan rubber to China's estimated civilian requirements of 2,500 tons per month.[4] This compromise—which failed to satisfy Churchill—was abandoned only a month later. As part of a general move to bring British policy more into line with that of the United States following the dismissal of MacArthur, rubber exports were suspended early in May, and remained suspended for the rest of the war.[5] Finally, on 25 June, and following the United Nations resolution of 18 May which urged an embargo on all military and strategic items, the Government began controlling by export licence all goods sent to China and Hong Kong. Similar arrangements were made in British dependent territories including Hong Kong itself.[6]

Nevertheless, in non-strategic materials and merchandise the China trade was maintained. It was encouraged by successive governments, Conservative as well as Labour, and its expansion pressed for by the Left and by business interests. The subject remained a matter of contention between British and American opinion.[7] American critics ranged from those who simply held

[1] H.C. Debs. Vol. 483. Col. *148* (1 February 1951).
[2] Ibid. Vol. 487. Col. *67* (25 April 1951).
[3] The licensing difficulty was officially given as the reason for allowing the rubber exports to continue (see Attlee, ibid., Col. 1429, 3 May 1951) but there would seem to be no adequate reason why the Government should not have stopped them by administrative action as eventually they did.
[4] Ibid. Col. 1592 (7 May 1951).
[5] Ibid. Cols. 1593, 1595, 1598 (7 May), 2180–82 and 2187 (10 May).
[6] Ibid. Vol. 489. Cols. 245–52 (19 June).
[7] One diplomatic correspondent considered that the China trade was the biggest single factor in Anglo–American differences during the Korean War. See the article by Michael Hilton, *Daily Telegraph*, 24 July 1953.

that any export to China was helpful to the Communist cause, to Senator McCarthy with his charge that Britain was carrying on a 'blood trade' with Peking. These attacks were the more resented in Britain when it was learned not only that the United States authorities had permitted Japan to trade with China, but that the United States herself, while banning all exports, had been importing from China considerably more than Britain, and that such imports were paid for in hard currency with which the Chinese could purchase war materials elsewhere.[1] Moreover, although Britain's China trade was inconsiderable when compared with her total trade, there was some feeling that the severity of American protective tariffs and the American 'hogging' of raw materials following the outbreak of the Korean War—a grievance which partly determined Attlee to visit Truman in December 1950—gave Britain the moral right to trade with whomsoever she could.[2] In short, much of the trouble was not simply political, but born of the economic jealousies and pressures—never far below the political surface where highly commercial and competitive powers are concerned—which already in the Far Eastern Crisis had helped to prevent a joint Anglo–American approach to the problems of post-war China and to the question of recognition.[3]

Whereas, during the last two years of the war, American opinion seems to have been exercised chiefly over the iniquitous British China trade, interest in Britain was centred mainly upon the

---

[1] American imports from Communist China in 1952 totalled $29 million, some three and a half times the British figure of £3 million. See: U.S. Department of Commerce, Bureau of the Census, *Quarterly Summary of Foreign Commerce of the United States*, June 1953, p. 3; H.C. Debs. Vol. 521. Cols. 348–9 (25 November 1953), Col. 1781 (8 December 1953).

[2] See: *New York Times*, London correspondent, 27 May 1951; Attlee, article in *Foreign Affairs*, January 1954.

[3] The readiness with which British suspicions were aroused is shown in the fairly common belief that the Americans had been selling cars to the Chinese through Japan. The few Britons who visited Peking during or shortly after the Korean War reported seeing numbers of American cars there, although in Washington it was stated that none had been sent to China since 1950 and only seven in 1949. See *The Times*, 4 November and 4 December 1953. It was even suggested that they were imported and paraded with the object of creating anti-American feeling in Britain. In fact many, perhaps all, of these cars had been imported before the Revolution.

possibility that the Americans might try to force an armistice by a more drastic use of their air superiority or by reviving Mac-Arthur's plan for attacking China. Following the dismissal of MacArthur, and the readjustment of British policy in June 1951, there would seem to be fewer grounds for a periodic display of Anglo–American irritability; nevertheless, that this still resulted must largely be accounted for by domestic developments in the two countries.

In the Anglo–American world, the Republicans, the American Government, the British Government and the British Left, represented on Far Eastern questions four different positions. The most serious situation was one involving an actual or potential rift between the two governments, as occurred during the winter crisis of 1950–51. A drawing together of the governments, however, did not diminish the clamour in the wings. On the contrary, it usually stimulated it. Through much of 1951 and the whole of 1952, the wings were especially clamorous; the onset of the presidential election campaign and the defeat of the Labour Government and emergence of the Bevanite faction also made them less easy to dismiss.

A stir was caused in Britain at the beginning of 1952 when Republican Party leaders gave the impression that they were not simply content with a policy of containment in the Far East, but favoured an offensive against Communism. On 22 January, Dulles, who although a Republican had then an official position in the State Department, expressed the hope that one day China might be freed from the Communists. On 10 February he declared that the United States should not stand by while any part of the world remained under Communist or Fascist dictatorship and that she should 'take the wraps off' Chiang Kai-shek's forces in Formosa. Similar speeches were made by Taft and Stassen, contenders for the Republican nomination. Stassen pressed for the return of MacArthur and advocated the immediate employment of Nationalist troops against the mainland. In Britain, liberal and radical opinion expressed great concern, the views of Dulles, Taft and Stassen being attacked both in Parliament and the press.[1] No doubt

---

[1] See: H.C. Debs. Vols. 495 and 496. Foreign affairs debate of 5 and 26 February 1952; Attlee, party political broadcast, report in *The Times*, 25 February; Harold Wilson, speech at Coventry, report in the *Observer*,

there was much genuine apprehension, but the impact on the British Left of these primarily electioneering speeches had another side to it. Criticism of American belligerency or recklessness had now become an issue in British domestic politics.

Until the spring of 1951, the Labour Left, although frequently vociferous and occasionally rebellious, did not represent a serious challenge to official foreign policy. So long as Aneurin Bevan remained in the cabinet, the Left had no one of major political stature to rally to. So long, too, as Ernest Bevin remained Foreign Secretary, official policy had as its advocate and defender probably the most considerable political figure in the whole Labour movement. Moreover, on all major issues of foreign policy the Government had the firm backing of the Opposition. Bevin's replacement as Foreign Secretary in March and his death in April, the resignation of Bevan and Wilson in April, and finally the defeat of the Labour Government in October 1951, inevitably altered the balance of forces within the Labour Party. The cohesion imposed by responsibility was largely lost, and the Left-wing of the Party, always happier in opposition, became an increasing trouble to the leadership.

For Bevan, the Western and particularly American approach to the Far Eastern Crisis, was both morally wrong and tactically foolish. Like most radicals he saw the Communist revolution as basically a protest movement of the ordinary people. 'Most British workers,' he said on one occasion, 'if they were in China, would be Chinese Communists.'[1] That Communism presented a threat he did not deny, but that it was primarily a military threat he considered a dangerous delusion. Holding the Communist means of expansion to be chiefly economic and social, he maintained that only in the same field could the challenge be adequately met. He distrusted American leadership and saw American rearmament as simply increasing the risk of war.

I am not anti-American [he said at Jarrow on 16 March 1952] ... but I do not believe that the American nation has the experience, sagacity, or the self-restraint necessary for world leadership at this

---

17 February; *Manchester Guardian*, leading articles, 19 January and 14 February; *Daily Herald*, leading articles, 13 and 14 February; *Observer*, leading article, 17 February; *News Chronicle*, column by A. J. Cummings, 19 February.

[1] Speech at Leith, 30 March 1952. *Scotsman*, 31 March.

time. They are engaged in the greatest rearmament programme the world has ever seen, and I cannot see any sense in it.[1]

In consequence he held that Britain should exert all her influence to have American policy changed or modified.[2] Her bargaining power for doing so was, he thought, greater than was generally admitted.[3]

Taken as a whole, these views represented a marked departure from the line adopted by the Labour Government in June 1951. Even so, as an expression of Left-wing opinion they were comparatively moderate, others, notably R. H. S. Crossman, wanting a foreign policy entirely independent of America's. In these circumstances the leadership could not afford to support Conservative policy as the Conservatives had supported Bevin's. It had, if a defection of the Left was to be guarded against, to move a little to the Left itself. Nor, in terms of the national interest, did this seem altogether uncalled for. Churchill's, to some, exaggerated concern for Anglo–American harmony and his reputed partiality for adventurous and bellicose policies (he had never before served as prime minister in peace time) were also reasons why the Opposition might have felt obliged to pull the other way.

The result was that American indiscretions, whether verbal or military, were used as a stick with which to beat a supposedly acquiescent Government. The pattern was set by the foreign affairs debate of 5 February 1952. Labour members sought to show, by referring to the American press and the statements of certain service chiefs, that pressure for a war with China was growing, and that during his visit to Washington the previous month Churchill had done nothing to discourage these tendencies; that in fact, in addressing Congress, he had himself made a provocative speech in which he had not only expressed satisfaction that the Americans were guarding Formosa, but declared that if a Korean armistice was concluded and then broken, the reply would be 'prompt, resolute and effective'.[4] From such a speech, said Attlee, the Americans would assume that there was to be a change in British policy; Churchill had

---

[1] *The Times*, 17 March 1952.
[2] Speech in London, 23 November 1952. *Daily Telegraph*, 24 November.
[3] See 'Our Great Debate', article in the *New Statesman*, 19 May 1951.
[4] *Documents on International Affairs, 1952*, p. 49.

tried to please his audience; he had implied support for Chiang Kai-shek and had made only one reference to the United Nations.[1] That night Attlee and other Labour front-benchers tabled a motion which censured Churchill personally for his 'failure to give adequate expression to [British] policy in the course of his recent visit to the United States'.[2]

Before the debate could be resumed on the following day, the sudden death of King George VI brought all business to a standstill. Much interest had, however, been aroused, largely because Churchill had apparently committed Britain to possible future action against China. Indeed the *Daily Worker*, although in this it was alone, showed its vexation that so important a matter should have been put off by the sovereign's demise. When the debate was renewed three weeks later on 26 February, the Opposition assailed the Government with quotations from some of the wilder speeches that the Republican leaders had managed to make in the meantime. Although this may have been one way of showing a potential Republican administration that at least half of Britain was vehemently opposed to their schemes, it showed too that for a censure motion the Opposition had little to go upon. In fact Churchill had no difficulty in demolishing the case against him. He declared that he was opposed to Chinese embroilments, and had always made this clear:

I have argued since the beginning of these troubles that nothing could be more foolish than for the armies of the United States or the United Nations to be engulfed in the vast areas of China, and also that few adventures could be less successful or fruitful than for Generalissimo Chiang Kai-shek to plunge on to the mainland.[3]

Moreover, with regard to the promise of 'prompt, resolute and effective' retaliation, which had so excited Labour backbenchers, he brought off a parliamentary *coup* by revealing that Attlee and Morrison had themselves agreed, in May 1951, to action 'not confined to Korea' if the Chinese should mount heavy air attacks from beyond the Yalu, and in September, to measures of a more limited character if a breakdown of the truce talks were followed by heavy fighting.[4] Not surprisingly the Opposition lost credit in the eyes of the impartial. The

---

[1] H.C. Debs. Vol. 495. Cols. 835–41.   [2] *The Times*, 6 February 1952.
[3] H.C. Debs. Vol. 496. Col. 982.   [4] Ibid. Cols. 968–78.

Manchester Guardian spoke of the Labour leaders' pressing the matter to a debate as an 'amazing action', an attempt to appease the Left by running with every anti-American hare; to the *Observer* the debate was 'deplorable' and the China question now as much the plaything of British politics as of American.[1]

The following June the Opposition reacted in much the same way, although with more justification, over the bombing by the Americans of the Yalu power stations. Situated near the Korean frontier, and supplying power to Manchuria besides North Korea, these installations had not been interfered with since MacArthur's retreat of December 1950. News of the raid, the biggest of the war, greatly excited Labour members in the Commons, and Attlee demanded an immediate debate on a matter of urgent public importance. This the Speaker disallowed, but on the following day, 25 June, the Opposition arranged a debate in the Supply Committee.[2] Labour speakers were severely critical of the American action chiefly because they thought it would endanger rather than speed up the truce talks which had by then reached a critical stage. The Chinese, they held, might well react violently to a blow which was aimed as much at them as at the North Koreans; had they not entered the war partly to protect these power stations upon which much of their industry depended? Furthermore, the bombing represented a change of policy about which the British Government had not been consulted. Apart from Lord Hinchingbrooke who argued that there were only two ways of ending a war, by surrender or by truce, and that a truce was not obtained by the processes of war, Conservative speakers in general disagreed that the raid was unjustified or that it would jeopardize the truce talks. But they were resentful that the American authorities had not informed the British Government beforehand. Failure to notify the Minister of Defence, Field-Marshal Lord Alexander, even though he had but recently visited the American Command in Korea, was regarded as particularly remiss.

Nevertheless, one can detect both in this debate, and in that

---

[1] *Manchester Guardian*, 28 February; *Observer*, 2 March 1952.

[2] H.C. Debs. Vol. 502. Cols. 2247–308, 2332–69. When the House debates Supply, the Opposition has in practice the choice of subject.

which followed on 1 July[1]—when the Opposition moved a motion of censure against the Government for failing to secure effective consultation with the Americans—a greater underlying agreement between the two front benches, than between each and its Tory or Socialist wing respectively. Whereas a number of Conservative back-benchers took the American view that a few hard knocks would make the Chinese readier to conclude a truce, leaders of the Government apparently thought the bombing unwise on political grounds but felt obliged to back up the American Government once the thing had been done.[2] On the Labour side the differences were more apparent. The leaders would almost certainly have acted as their opposite numbers had they still been in office, but it was a course which was far from satisfying to the Bevanites. These complained that the censure motion was far too moderate.[3] Moreover, they fiercely attacked United States policy which they held to be intransigent and increasingly militaristic. There was something to be said on either side. The Left assumed too readily that a burnt-out war had suddenly been poked into flame. In fact, although less publicized than formerly, vigorous fighting had been proceeding all the time, so that from the military angle, the raid was neither irrelevant nor particularly provocative. On the other hand, it is usually wiser to put up with a military disadvantage than to take an undoubted political risk. In taking such a risk the Americans revealed an attitude to war which has always caused difficulties with the British when the two nations have fought as allies. Chester Wilmot has described it in his history of the European campaign of 1944–5:

Since America fights for no political objective, except peace, no political directions should be given to American commanders in the field. They should be completely free to determine their strategy on military grounds alone, and the supreme military consideration is to bring hostilities to an end. To pursue a political aim is to practise Imperialism.[4]

---

[1] H.C. Debs. Vol. 503. Cols. 255–380.   [2] See Healey, ibid. Col. 353.

[3] According to *The Times* Parliamentary correspondent, at a private meeting of the Parliamentary Labour Party held shortly before the debate of 1 July, the Bevanites pressed for a motion condemning the bombing, but were outvoted by 102 to 51. A large abstention suggests much tacit support for the minority view. See *The Times*, 2 July.

[4] Chester Wilmot. *The Struggle for Europe*, pp. 714–15.

Although, since then, the Americans had been forced by events to pay more attention to the political aspects of war, this tradition died hard—if indeed it is dead even yet–especially amongst the military. In the case of the Yalu bombing it is not entirely surprising that although the power stations were regarded as having a special political significance—they had been the subject of discussions between Acheson and Morrison in September, and were on the agreed list of targets if the truce talks should break down and give way to heavy fighting—the Secretary of State knew nothing of the attack until it had taken place. He himself attributed both this, and the failure to inform the British, to an administrative mistake, but had the political aspects of the raid been given adequate attention by those planning it, such a mistake could hardly have occurred.[1]

Altogether this military bias of the Americans was an important factor in the crises in Anglo–American relations which arose over Far East affairs. That it existed was sufficient to cause uneasiness. That it was over-stressed was scarcely surprising given the Americans' liking for tough talk and action, and their un-English habit of popularizing the vicious side of war.[2] A Marshall or an Eisenhower might be widely and deservedly popular, but in radical and Left-wing circles particularly, the American military as a whole were viewed with antipathy and suspicion. The detached manner in which certain generals and admirals advocated or contemplated the liberation of the Communist world by force, the pressure in military circles for aid to, and bases in, countries under Fascist or reactionary régimes, and the development and use by the American services of the most frightful weapons ever devised, all helped to create a picture of a cold, amoral professionalism. The United States army and navy were quasi-political organizations, jealous, competitive, and to the British mind, much too independent. The Defence and State Departments also, seemed often to be at loggerheads, and, of the two, the latter under Acheson had the better reputation in Britain. Indeed, 'the

[1] See: *Christian Science Monitor*, Washington correspondent, 9 July 1952; H.C. Debs. Vol. 503. Cols. 277 and 361 (1 July 1952).

[2] In November 1951 an issue of *Collier's* magazine devoted entirely to World War III—which the Americans win after atom-bombing Moscow—achieved a certain notoriety in Left-wing circles.

Pentagon' came to be used almost as a bogy term by the British Left. It is against this background that we must view criticism of American military policy in Korea. This was not confined to the Yalu raid, or to the employment, condemned by church-men and other humanitarians, of the notorious napalm bomb.[1] Many had come to believe that the negotiations at Panmun-jom were not bearing fruit largely owing to American rigidity and stubbornness, that, in fact, the American military were by no means eager for a truce on equitable terms.

Over the issue which was chiefly holding up the truce—whether or not prisoners of war should be repatriated against their will—there was almost universal agreement in Britain that the large numbers of Chinese and North Korean prisoners who refused to go back should not be forced to do so, even if this meant a continuation of the war. On the other hand, many felt that a truce would not be difficult to obtain if the United Nations were prepared to make concessions in other directions. In some quarters it was held that something should be done about Formosa: the United States should disavow Chiang Kai-shek, or the promise of the island's return to China should be reaffirmed.[2] The immediate admission of Communist China to the United Nations was also increasingly urged and became once more official Labour policy.[3] Naturally most of this pres-sure came from the Left. In speech after speech Aneurin Bevan

---

[1] The napalm bomb usually burns to death every living thing it happens to drop near. Amongst those who condemned its use were the Archbishop of York and the radical Bishop of Birmingham. The latter (Dr. Barnes) des-cribed it as a greater disgrace to mankind than the atomic bomb; see *The Times*, 3 March 1952. It may here be pointed out, however, that except amongst fellow-travellers, Communist accusations that the Americans had engaged in bacteriological raids over China, received little or no credence. Left-wing opinion might well have harboured doubts about American guiltlessness but for Peking's refusal to allow an independent investigation. When in July 1952 the Dean of Canterbury (Dr. Hewlett Johnson) whose admiration for Communism had long been wholly uncritical, arrived from China with an immense amount of 'proof'—chiefly in the form of a huge roll of Chinese signatures—the nation's sense of humour seems to have got the better of its sense of horror. See the Lords' debate on the Dean's activi-ties, H.L. Debs. Vol. 177. Cols. 1116–64 (15 July 1952).

[2] See: letter from Lord Boyd-Orr, James Johnson, Marcus Lipton, Lady Selwyn-Clarke, Reginald Sorensen and Lord Stansgate (Labour M.P.s and other public figures), *The Times*, 29 August 1952; speech by John Strachey at Dundee, *News Chronicle*, 10 November 1952.   [3] See above, p. 64.

declared that there was small hope of peace while the United States persisted in supporting Chiang Kai-shek, but that if it was prepared to accept the Chinese Communist revolution as an accomplished fact, there would be 'a Korean truce to-morrow'.[1] Such suggestions were not very practical when set against an American casualty list then totalling over 100,000 and the state of feeling that this had helped to engender. Nevertheless they reflected a growing impatience throughout the country with the interminable negotiations, now genuine, now propagandist, at Panmunjom.

The war ended on a note of irritation and acrimony. The foundations of the armistice were really laid at the diplomatic level, the Soviet and Indian governments helping as inter-mediaries, but it was upon the situation in Korea itself that public attention was inevitably centred. After a lapse the truce talks were resumed in April 1953. Almost at once the chief American negotiator, General Harrison, came under sharp Labour and Liberal attack for intransigence and haggling over details. One Labour M.P. was for court-martialling him if such tactics caused the truce to be delayed.[2] The *Manchester Guardian* deplored the effect upon Asia.[3] Lord Samuel suggested that the negotiations should be taken over by statesmen—a step also urged by the *News Chronicle* and *Daily Herald*.[4] In the Commons, Attlee declared that there were elements in the United States wanting an all-out war with China; he suggested that the truce delegation should not consist solely of Americans, but that representatives of others of the allies should be included.[5] Public opinion polls revealed that this view was widely shared in the country, as also was the dissatisfaction with the way the negotiations were being handled.[6]

[1] E.g.: at Dalry, Ayrshire, report in the *Observer*, 15 June 1952; at a mass rally at Filey, *Daily Telegraph*, 17 June; in London, ibid., 24 November; at a mass May Day rally at Edinburgh of 100,000 miners and their families, *The Times*, 5 May 1953.

[2] Desmond Donnelly speaking at Didcot, *Daily Herald*, 4 May 1953.

[3] *Manchester Guardian*, 5 May.

[4] Speech at a United Nations Association meeting, *The Times*, 20 May; *News Chronicle*, 7 May and *Daily Herald*, 8 May.

[5] H.C. Debs. Vol. 515. Cols. 1065–6 (12 May). See also speeches by other Labour members during this Foreign Affairs debate of 11–12 May.

[6] See Appendix III, D15–16.

It may be argued that these strictures were not wholly merited. If Harrison was hard-bitten, so too were the Communists. They contested stubbornly every point and used military pressure to increase their bargaining strength. In such circumstances, any impatience for a settlement would undoubtedly have been taken advantage of. A more pliable negotiator might have succeeded more quickly, but less well. Nevertheless, because there were forces working against a Korean peace, there was much to be said, once the Communists had given way over the repatriation of prisoners (which they did following the death of Stalin in March) for a speedy settlement even at the cost of concessions over details. It was probably this consideration which made the Government critical, although not openly, of Harrison's conduct of the talks.[1] As it was, late in June when the negotiations were virtually complete, Syngman Rhee attempted to wreck the truce—and so preserve some hope of getting the United States to unify Korea by force —by allowing some 27,000 anti-Communist prisoners to escape. This strategem, which almost succeeded in its purpose,[2] caused an outcry in Britain, and not only on the Left. In the Commons Churchill twice used the word 'treachery', and the *Economist* suggested that it might be necessary to remove Rhee in the interests of peace.

The conclusion of the armistice on 27 July 1953 was greeted in Britain with reserved relief. No modern war had taken so long to wind up or had left so much unsettled, and the initial enthusiasm of taking part in a great international cause had largely evaporated when the United Nations decided to invade the invader. Nevertheless, satisfaction was generally felt that over the prisoner issue the right and humane thing had been done, and that in the successful resistance to aggression the worst errors of the 'thirties had been avoided.

[1] *Observer*, diplomatic correspondent, 17 May 1953.
[2] Eden, *Full Circle*, p. 27.

VIII

The Crisis in Indo-China

With the Korean War at an end, Indo-China became the chief centre of crisis in the Far East. The war there between the French and the Communist Vietminh movement had been proceeding since 1946, but not until its last months did it attain to any great international importance. The Korean armistice, however, allowed both China and the Western powers to take a much more active interest in the affairs of South-East Asia, and a powerful offensive launched by the Vietminh in December 1953 soon brought matters to a head.

So far as Britain is concerned, the story of the Indo-China crisis is primarily a diplomatic one. Between the British and American governments important differences of view arose as to what should be done. These, as well as the even more serious differences which had to be overcome if peace was to be restored, were resolved largely by British efforts. An account of the exchanges and negotiations, both inter-allied, and then between the two sides at the Geneva Conference, has been given at length by Sir Anthony Eden in his *Memoirs*.[1] Of controversy at home there was little. Indeed, there was almost unanimous support for the Government in the course which it followed. This is not to say that there were not differences of view and of emphasis, especially in the early stages. But these were overshadowed and overtaken by a general recognition that the best, in fact the only sensible, course for the Western powers was to try and get a compromise peace as in Korea.

This conclusion was assisted by the fact that there were many in Britain, particularly on the Left, who regarded the Vietminh with divided feelings. That it was important to prevent Communist infiltration into the rest of South-East Asia was generally acknowledged, but the Vietminh was also a nationalist movement fighting in the cause of Asian independence. In some

[1] Eden, *Full Circle*, Book I, Chapters V and VI, pp. 77–145. See also Coral Bell, *Survey of International Affairs, 1954*, Part I Crisis in Asia, pp. 12–73.

measure, therefore, it had the sympathy of British radicals, especially as these took a much poorer view of French than of British colonial rule and policy. In a foreign affairs debate in the Commons on 11 and 12 May 1953, every Labour speaker who referred to Indo-China stressed the necessity for an early French withdrawal and the granting of full independence. Had this been done earlier, Attlee argued, Ho Chi Minh (the leader of the Vietminh) might well have become prime minister as had happened with nationalist leaders in the Commonwealth.[1] Those on the Left of the Party strongly emphasized the nationalist character of the movement:

It is time to tell the French and the Americans [said R. H. S. Crossman] that they are fighting an unjust war in Indo-China. If the French had done the right thing, Indo-China today would stand alongside Indonesia and Burma. Ho Chi Minh and his rebels are not Communist by nature but by compulsion. They are driven to be Communists in order to get national liberation.[2]

Tory opinion was less favourably disposed to national liberation movements under Communist control, but since the time of the Chinese Civil War it had at least become more cognizant of their nationalist as distinct from their Communist character, and hence of the nature of their strength and appeal. By the end of 1953 practically no one in Britain believed that the French could win the Indo-China war, however much material and financial aid they received from the Americans.

The weeks immediately prior to the Geneva Conference, which, from 26 April 1954, was to attempt to settle the future of both Indo-China and Korea, were marked by a number of Anglo–American disagreements. In fact each government saw the coming conference in a different light. Eden, anxious for a negotiated peace, and in favour of partition as a solution that stood a chance of being accepted and of lasting, had eagerly taken up Molotov's idea of a five-power meeting that included Communist China, when first it was mooted at the Berlin Conference in January. Dulles, however, who viewed the participation of Communist China with repugnance, had agreed to the idea only after every effort had been made, chiefly by the British, to meet his reservations and objections. Moreover, being

---

[1] H.C. Debs. Vol. 515. Col. 1068 (12 May 1953).
[2] Ibid. Col. 1122. See also M. Foot, Cols. 950–1 (11 May).

opposed to partition he seems to have set little store by the conference except in so far as it might provide the Western powers with an opportunity to negotiate from strength and get a solution to their liking. Only a short while before, on 12 January, he had propounded the principle of 'massive and instant retaliation' as an answer to any form of Communist aggression. Although widely criticized and subsequently qualified, this really signified an increase of confidence resulting from American development of the hydrogen bomb and of tactical atomic weapons.[1] Thus, before the conference began, Dulles felt that the time had come to make a demonstration of Western unity and resolve. On 29 March he declared that the imposition of Communism on South-East Asia

should not be passively accepted but should be met by united action. This might involve serious risks, but these risks are far less than those that will face us in a few years from now if we dare not be resolute today.[2]

A few days later he proposed that the Western powers should warn China of their readiness to take concerted action against her if she continued to aid and abet the Vietminh. The third and most serious suggestion came on the very eve of the Geneva Conference. It was that the United States and United Kingdom should attempt to save the besieged French fortress of Dien Bien Phu, the fall of which was imminent, by immediate air intervention.

News of this last proposal, and of the British Cabinet's rejection of it on 25 April, was not made public in Britain until 30 April when, following a report in the *New York Herald Tribune*, it caused something of a sensation. There could, indeed, be no doubt that the bulk of British opinion was firmly against armed intervention. On 12 April Labour M.P.s, suspicious of possible commitments in Indo-China, had closely questioned the Government about Dulles's proposal for concerted action.[3] Churchill's statement on 27 April that the Government had not undertaken any military commitments, and would not do

---

[1] See Coral Bell, *Survey of International Affairs, 1954*, Part II Armaments, pp. 98–102. The Americans tested several hydrogen bombs in the Pacific in March and April 1954.

[2] Eden, *Full Circle*, p. 91.

[3] H.C. Debs. Vol. 526. Cols. 784–7.

K

so while the Geneva Conference was in being,[1] was widely welcomed. On 28 April, with the plight of Dien Bien Phu by now
desperate, the Labour Party declared itself unreservedly against
intervention when its national executive committee adopted
the following resolution:

The national executive committee of the Labour Party is strongly
opposed to any step which would involve Britain in military action
in support of imperialist policies in Indo-China. It reaffirms its
opposition to any extension of hostilities which might lead to a
major war. . . .[2]

Press comment was almost uniformly of the same opinion, and
a Gallup Poll taken in May showed that not only military but
also naval and air intervention was opposed by an overwhelming majority.[3]

If British opinion found little to commend in the Dulles proposals, this was not simply owing to radical sympathy for Asian
nationalism, or fear that, if adopted, they could lead to world
war; they were also considered to be militarily and politically
unsound. With Congress hostile to the employment of American
troops in Indo-China, intervention would have to be confined to
air attacks. And Korea had plainly shown that even total air
superiority could not of itself determine the issue on the ground.
Thus Dulles was widely regarded as adopting a foolish policy of
bluff—foolish because, had the bluff been called, there was no
apparent means, short of strategic atomic bombing, of backing
it up. The Chinese, said the *Manchester Guardian* on 7 May,
could quickly put half a million troops into Indo-China, whereas the Americans and British had nothing available nearer than
California and Suez. The Government had taken the same
view. To Churchill the proposal for joint action was an invitation to take part in an ineffective military operation which
could bring the world to the verge of a major war. He and
Eden considered that more was to be gained by keeping the
Chinese guessing as to Western intentions.[4] On the political side
the objections were equally cogent. Had the joint warning been
made or the policy of intervention been carried out, the Geneva
Conference would most likely never have met, let alone suc-

---

[1] Ibid. Cols. 1455–6.   [2] *The Times*, 29 April 1954.
[3] See Appendix III, E4–5.   [4] Eden, *Full Circle*, p. 105.

ceeded. Apart from putting an end to any hopes of settling the Indo-China crisis by negotiation, this would have made a very bad impression throughout Asia. If the Conference in any case proved sterile, steps would have to be taken for the collective defence of South-East Asia. In the British view, however, any such arrangement would be meaningless unless it enjoyed the support of independent Asia, and of India in particular. This, it was believed, would hardly be forthcoming if the West was primarily responsible for breaking up the Conference. Any intransigence must clearly be shown as coming from the Communist side.[1]

Unfortunately, India proved to be a further source of Anglo–American disagreement. In American eyes, by her neutralism and refusal to help share the United Nations military burden in Korea, she had forfeited any right to special consideration. In Britain, where the Asian outlook was better appreciated, not only was India's benevolent neutrality regarded as a piece of good fortune for the West, but her mediation would, it was thought, contribute materially to any success that might be achieved. Thus in August 1953 the British had pressed hard for India to be represented at the Korean Political Conference, but the Americans had mustered enough votes to defeat the proposal. This action had been widely resented in Britain, particularly as the Indians had successfully supervised the tricky prisoner-of-war exchanges and given much diplomatic help over the truce. Indeed, on this occasion every national newspaper with the exception of the *Daily Express* (which had long had an aversion to Nehru and his policies) took the side of India as against the United States. For the Right this was certainly a departure from the attitude adopted over recognition, and the shift of view was equally apparent during the Indo-China crisis. There is no doubt that on the Right there was less prejudice against India than formerly, as well as a more realistic view of Asian nationalism in general.

But it was also true that with Dulles as Secretary of State, there was not the same Anglo–American harmony as during the Truman Administration. Despite occasional disagreements

[1] See: leading articles of the *Observer*, 11 April, *Scotsman*, 12 April, *News Chronicle*, 19 April, and *Manchester Guardian*, 7 May; report by Drew Middleton, *New York Times*, 23 May.

and the trouble sometimes caused by the irresponsible utterances of officials, the British Government always knew where it stood with Truman and Acheson. But with Dulles it did not always know. Even before he became Secretary of State, he had earned a reputation for unreliability in British official circles over the affair of the 'Yoshida letter'. When negotiating the Japanese peace treaty in June 1951, Dulles apparently assured Morrison, who was then Foreign Secretary, that no American pressure would be put upon the Japanese to recognize the Chinese Nationalists. Yet the following January, Yoshida, the Japanese prime minister, wrote to Dulles in terms which strongly suggested that such pressure had been applied.[1] As a result of this, Morrison 'resolved then and there not fully to trust Dulles again'.[2] Eden too, several times experienced the same lack of dependability. In April 1954 Dulles informed Eden that he was against the inclusion of India in his proposed security system for South-East Asia, and that any attempt to bring her in would be countered by the inclusion of Formosa. However, at Eden's insistence he agreed that the whole question of membership should be discussed with the Indian and other governments beforehand. Yet within three days the Secretary of State had invited to a meeting in Washington the representatives of his own choice of powers, India being excluded. In a message to the British ambassador in Washington, Eden wrote:

Americans may think the time past when they need consider the feelings or difficulties of their allies. It is the conviction that this tendency becomes more pronounced every week that is creating mounting difficulties for anyone in this country who wants to maintain close Anglo-American relations. We, at least, have constantly to bear in mind all our Commonwealth partners, even if the United States does not like some of them . . .[3]

This somewhat bitter comment is but a further indication of the extent to which even a Conservative Government found

---

[1] See: Eden, *Full Circle*, pp. 19–20; Leon D. Epstein, *Britain—Uneasy Ally*, pp. 228–9.

[2] Lord Morrison of Lambeth, *Herbert Morrison: An Autobiography*, p. 280.

[3] Eden, *Full Circle*, p. 99. On the difficulty of dealing with Dulles, see pp. 63–4.

itself out of sympathy with official American policies and attitudes since the Republicans entered office.

That the Government intended to examine the possibility of a collective defence scheme for South-East Asia was revealed by Eden in the Commons on 13 April. Reactions were mixed. The idea had appealed to the Government in principle, first because the area was vulnerable to Communist penetration, and secondly because any resultant treaty would supersede the ANZUS Pact from which Britain was unwillingly and embarrassingly excluded.[1] Some of the Labour leaders favoured the proposal for the same reasons. The Labour Party, declared Gaitskell on 15 May, had no reason to oppose the idea in principle; it was fully in keeping with past policy, and the fact of Communist imperialism in South-East Asia had to be faced.[2] George Brown, who as shadow Minister of Defence was to be one of Gaitskell's strongest supporters in the defence controversies which convulsed the Labour Party in 1960-1, argued similarly. Writing in the *Daily Herald* on 23 April, he looked forward to a defence system which would be as important as NATO. On 20 June he urged that SEATO should be set up without delay, that Anglo–American differences should be resolved, and that a line should be drawn through South-East Asia which the Communists would be forbidden to cross.[3]

In contrast, many of those on the Left of the Party were strongly opposed to a defence arrangement which they saw as a means of battening down American influence upon peoples who simply wanted to be left alone. Bevan described Eden's announcement as a surrender to American pressure, and the following day resigned from the shadow cabinet.[4] Writing in *Tribune*, he declared that if the United States persisted in the scheme, she should be told 'to go it alone'. Another vigorous and persistent critic was the *Manchester Guardian*. It spoke of Eden's statement as 'surprising and disturbing', asked what good such a

---

[1] Ibid., p. 93.

[2] Speech at Ampthill, Bedfordshire. *Observer*, 16 May.

[3] Speech at Belper, Derbyshire. *Daily Telegraph*, 21 June.

[4] H.C. Debs. Vol. 526. Col. 971 (13 April). Although according to the political correspondent of the *Daily Telegraph* (27 April) Bevan's resignation was precipitated by disagreement with Attlee over SEATO, he had become increasingly out of sympathy with the policy of the leadership.

pact would do, and observed that there was no point in creating
a Pacific NATO when the situations in Europe and the Far
East were so unlike.[1]

In the event, the Government's handling of the SEATO
proposal disarmed most of the critics. Churchill made it clear
that the negotiations at Geneva had first priority and that no
final decisions would be taken until after the Conference, and
Eden was as eager as the Opposition that India and other
'Colombo Plan' countries should be consulted throughout and
invited to participate.[2] This put an end to the Dulles plan for
setting up immediately an anti-Communist alliance in order to
help save the situation in Indo-China, and also to much of the
hostility to SEATO which had begun to arise particularly in
India. With Geneva settled, the need for some form of permanent defensive arrangement for this area of small, unstable and
defenceless states was generally conceded. Even the *Manchester
Guardian*, on the day the conference ended, urged the establishment of SEATO despite Left-wing criticism.[3]

The diplomatic history of the Geneva Conference does not
properly concern this study. British policy throughout was
first to prevent the Conference from breaking up, and
secondly to obtain a settlement that would leave no more than
the northern half of Vietnam in Communist hands. In the face
of great difficulties—the intransigence of the Chinese, the weakness of the French, and the periodic desire of the Americans to
abandon the Conference and resort to intervention—Eden succeeded in both these aims.

In his efforts he had the encouragement, and in his achievements the congratulations, of an almost united country. It was
to be noticed, however, that the Right tended to be less satisfied
with the terms of the settlement than the Left. Although Tory

---

[1] *Manchester Guardian*, 14 April.

[2] H.C. Debs. Vol. 527. Col. 1692 (17 May), Vol. 530. Col. 44 (12
July).

[3] For public opinion of the SEATO proposal, see Appendix III, E8. The
South-East Asia Collective Defence Treaty was signed at Manila in Septem-
ber 1954, the 'Western' members being the United States, the United
Kingdom, France, Australia and New Zealand. Eden invited the five
'Colombo' powers of India, Pakistan, Ceylon, Burma and Indonesia to join,
but all except Pakistan declined. The only other Asian members were the
Philippines and Thailand.

opinion for the most part welcomed the ending of hostilities, the evacuation by the French of the whole of northern Vietnam including Hanoi and the Red River delta, was in some quarters looked upon as almost too high a price to pay, only to be justified by imperative necessity.[1] And for a few dissentients not even peace could excuse what they regarded as a Western scuttle: the *Daily Express*, true to its tradition of regarding the loss of any colony by whatsoever power, and howsoever governed, as unpardonable; Lord Vansittart, who observed that temporary and unreliable agreements with tyrannies were always possible provided one gave way enough; and *Punch*, which carried a cartoon of Eden dressed like Chamberlain; all denigrated the Geneva settlement. But these were lone voices, and few found Munich an apposite comparison.[2]

The Left, on the other hand, was enthusiastic. Pacifist and Left-wing members of the parliamentary Labour Party tabled motions warmly welcoming the settlement and expressing hopes for future negotiations. Partly they had Germany in mind, for they detested the idea of German rearmament and immediately clamoured for a further international conference on the subject. But more generally, Geneva, as they saw it, had vindicated a view they had been voicing for years: that if Britain broke free from American influence and approached the Communist powers in a conciliatory spirit, suspicions would be dispelled and the prospects for a peaceful future greatly improved. Yet it is possible to argue too much as too little from the success of Geneva. It was a settlement resulting from the weakness of the French and their Vietnamese allies. The Communists gained more than they had conquered at the price of calling off the war. Hence, unless the West was prepared to make similar concessions—as some of the Left would certainly have liked—there

[1] The *Daily Telegraph*, approximately constituency or back-bench Tory in outlook, at first regarded partition as 'intolerable' (20 April) and 'an unmitigated confession of defeat' if allowed (26 April), but later (12 and 15 July) accepted it as inevitable. The *Sunday Times* commented (2 May): 'Unless events compel it, a territorial partition would be a poor solution'.

[2] See: *Daily Express*, 21 July; Lord Vansittart, letter to *The Times*, 27 July; *Punch*, 19 May. Malcolm Muggeridge, the editor of *Punch*, who in 1956 took a leading part in opposing the visit of Khrushchev and Bulganin to Britain, defended the cartoon in the *News Chronicle* on 22 May, but prevailing press comment was that it was silly and mischievous.

was small hope that other outstanding differences could be
settled in the same way. That the Geneva Conference made
not the slightest headway on the question of Korea's political
future is surely indicative of this.[1] Moreover, until almost the
end of the Conference it was highly doubtful, in view of the
continuing military success of the Vietminh, that the Communists would agree to a settlement in Indo-China acceptable
to the West. Various reasons were suggested for their doing so,
amongst them the fear of alienating Asian opinion, and the
desire of the Russians not to weaken Mendès-France, a French
premier presumed to be against the proposed European Defence
Community.[2] Most probably, however, the simplest explanation is the true one. In view of the American attitude throughout, the almost certain alternative to a breakdown of the Conference would have been another Korea, leading at the worst
to world war, or at the best to an equitable partition after
a prolonged and pointless struggle. Thus Dulles, for all his
fumbling and lack of a coherent policy, had probably more
to do, though indirectly, with the positive results of Geneva
than the Left either realized or was prepared to give him credit
for.

Nevertheless, it would be wrong to regard Geneva as no more
than the logical answer to a potential power stalemate; it was
also both a justification and a fulfilment of British Far Eastern
policy since the war. That Britain recognized Communist
China made Eden's task easier, and probably saved the Conference at a time when the Americans and French had no personal contact with the other side. The ending of a colonial war
removed an irritant in relations between Asia and the West, and

---

[1] The Korean discussions soon ran into deadlock over the question of
what form the all-Korea elections were to take and how they should be
supervised. The Communists demanded a Supervisory Commission in
which they would, in effect, have a veto; their opponents insisted upon a
United Nations Commission as the only real guarantee of free elections. On
15 June the sixteen U.N. allies, recognizing the impossibility of agreement,
issued a statement setting forth their own case and recapitulating the
differences. Both sides made it clear, however, that they did not desire a
resumption of hostilities. See: *Survey of International Affairs, 1954*, Part VII 'The
Far East' by F. C. Jones, pp. 271–8; Guy Wint, *What Happened in Korea?*,
pp. 137–41.

[2] See *The Times*, 23 June and 21 July.

the lessening of tension reduced the risk that American attention and strength would be diverted to the Far East at the expense of Europe and the Middle East. If, therefore, British opinion was in general satisfied, the instinct was sound.

Conclusion

British opinion during the Far Eastern crisis may be appraised at three levels: at the level of political and moral predilection, at that of political responsibility, and at the international level. In the case of the first we have primarily to do with sentiment and principle, in the second with policy, and in the third with those opinions which being sufficiently national in their acceptance or expression, may be so at variance with those of another country as to affect relations with it.

From the time when the Chinese Communist Revolution became a subject of widespread interest and concern, there began to emerge a broad division of opinion in Britain about developments in the Far East and the policies the Western powers should pursue there. Partly this was owing to a genuine difference of view over what was best in the national interest— a difference which was eventually narrowed and finally resolved. But the division also reflected the conflicting traditions, philosophies, and sentiments which characterize British political life. On the one side were ranged those who see the international world as a community; on the other were those for whom it is primarily a scene of power, conflict, and self-preservation. Although some overlapping is inevitable, this division largely corresponds to that between Left and Right in domestic politics.

It is upon the subject of nationalism that their difference of outlook is perhaps most apparent. The Far Eastern Crisis was essentially an affair of two conflicts: that of Communist power versus Western power; and that of nationalism versus imperialism. So far as political and moral sentiments are concerned, the two groups were largely at one over the first conflict; the second divided them sharply.

Moreover, they were divided still further by the habitual tendency of each side to interpret a situation in terms of that conflict over which it feels the more strongly or about which there is widespread public concern. Thus the Right will often justify an attack upon hostile nationalism as a necessary preventive measure against Communism; the Left will tend to condemn any action directed against Communist power—at least as far as the newly emergent countries are concerned—as an onslaught by imperialism upon nationalism. And the more the political outlook is an expression not so much of an interest as of a faith, the more subjectively or even doctrinally determined will the political judgement usually be.

The views of the older generation of radical idealists upon Communist China, particularly in the period of its rise, afford an instance of this. Men like Lord Lindsay or Lord Samuel could hardly be described as political extremists, but they embodied the hopefulness and idealism that had been characteristic of an earlier and less uncompromising age. Supremely conscious of, and sympathetic towards, the needs of the masses for a better life, and firm believers in the principle of self-determination, they welcomed the Chinese Revolution much as they did the emancipation of India and of other Asian countries since the war. Also, being prone to ascribe international conflicts to misunderstandings and justifiable fears rather than to cynical calculation or implacable enmity, they were inclined, in the years which followed, to see the whole crisis in terms of a great nation's demanding, and to a large extent being denied, its legitimate rights. Even when the agrarian democrat interpretation of Chinese Communism was shown to be mistaken, and the hopes that Western interests in China would be protected were proved false, there were many who wished well of the new power, regarding the political, social and economic changes which resulted as representing an inevitable and necessary stage in China's historical development.

It was natural that those who held these views should have approached the problems of recognition, the Chinese seat, and the status of Formosa, largely as moralists. The withholding of Formosa from the Communists, despite the possibility of mass executions if control were to pass to the mainland, was for some, as for Lord Stansgate, primarily the dishonouring of a promise. Over the Chinese seat liberal and radical feeling was particularly strong. For many its denial to Peking was an unwarrantable interference with the right of a people to be represented, as well as a blow to their conception of the United Nations as a place where world conflicts might be resolved and ultimate world unity fostered.

These hopes and scruples were less characteristic of political opinion further to the Left, but here there was a greater feeling of ideological affinity with the revolutionary movements of Asia as well as a more widespread distrust of American intentions. Aneurin Bevan, who from April 1951 was the most prominent, although far from being the most extreme personality of the dissenting Left, declared that the British working class, were it living in a Chinese environment, would be Communist.[1] It was this type of sentiment which largely determined their attitude and affected their judgement.

Just how far, in some cases, it could be affected, was apparent during the opening phase of the Korean War. This was a conflict which it would be difficult objectively to describe as one of nationalism versus imperialism. Rather was it a plain encounter between Communist and Western power. Moreover, with the Communists having been the aggressors, and the United Nations having endowed the cause of Western resistance with its name and authority, it might be supposed that there would be little here to disturb even the most sensitive radical or Left-wing conscience. And indeed, the great majority, even those responsible for the publication of *Tribune*, declared their support for resistance. Yet there were some—S. O. Davies, G. D. H. Cole, K. Zilliacus, and others of the extreme Left—who saw the struggle primarily as that of the Korean people against American capitalism and militarism, and so favoured a Northern victory.

Compared with these expressions of liberal and Left-wing sentiment, the prevailing views of the Right were little publicized and so are more difficult to assess. Fewer Tories than radicals appear to have had illusions about agrarian democracy, and there was undoubtedly an earlier awareness on the Right of the growth of Communism and of the threat this presented to the interests and ultimately the security of the Western powers. The phenomenon, however, was largely misunderstood. Many Tories assigned too great a role to Moscow, believing the Asian Communist movements to be simply projections of Soviet influence. Nevertheless, partly because they saw the crisis largely in terms of Communist power politics, there was little tendency amongst Tories to criticize the political and strategic

[1] See p. 124 above.

measures adopted by the Americans to safeguard their position in the Far East. Even when MacArthur's policies appeared likely to lead to a general war, few Conservatives were disposed to censure him, and the Peace with China movement which was a product of the war-scare of the winter of 1950–1, remained predominantly radical and Left-wing in character.

In fact, attitudes towards the possibility of war with China, as towards the other questions and policies concerning her, were largely determined by the particular image of China adopted. For the liberal or radical, 'China' generally meant the hundreds of millions of ordinary Chinese, who had already suffered from more than twenty years of war and misrule, and for whom Communism simply meant the end of exploitation and pillage. Thus a war against China would be not only the supreme folly, but the supreme crime. For others, however, 'China' signified an evil ideology, G. F. Hudson's 'new marches of Xerxes to subdue Hellas', or Lord Vansittart's régime of brutes. To fight such a power, even if this were better avoided, might therefore be excusable; to give way to it could be regarded only as 'appeasement'—a confession of impotence and moral cowardice.

Naturally not everyone on the Right shared this particular point of view, nor was being a realist as well as a radical necessarily a contradiction in terms. Even in the months following the Chinese intervention in Korea, there were Tories who favoured a more conciliatory policy towards Communist China, just as there was a considerable body of Labour opinion that was clearly aware of the need to curb Communist expansion in Asia. Yet instinctively and emotionally the two sides were facing in opposite directions. Because they sympathized with and idealized its reforming and nationalist aspects, liberals and radicals all too often either ignored the Marxist–Leninist content of the Chinese Revolution, or failed to see its full significance. Indeed, even of those who knew China best, there were some who, believing that Chinese Communism was potentially more, and not less, liberal than Russian, adopted a view characteristic enough to be described in a novel satirizing post-war Britain:

The British are always prepared to believe that in a totalitarian State there exists a worthy class of people known as 'the moderates'. They believed this of Nazi Germany, they believed it of Japan in the 1930's. It is a belief which invariably deters them from doing anything remotely provocative, for they feel that they would thereby play into the hands of the extremists and weaken the influence of 'the moderates', who are always conceived to be well-intentioned, peace-loving and pro-British.[1]

If the Right made the same mistake, or used the same excuse, over the Fascist régimes of the 1930s, it certainly did not in the case of Communist China. Yet the inability of many Tories to see the Chinese Revolution other than in terms of Communist expansion or even, sometimes, of Soviet imperialism, suggests that in general the Right had but little comprehension of the nature and force of post-war Asian nationalism, and notably of the behaviour of a proud and ancient people in violent reaction against the century-old dominance of the Western powers.

To what extent did these political and moral predilections affect opinion at the level of political responsibility? Certainly the foreign policy of the Labour Government had its idealistic side. Ernest Bevin, in justifying his efforts to bring Peking into the United Nations, declared that the Government tried not to become obsessed with the Communist conception of China, remembering that the mass of Chinese scarcely understood what Communism was. Other cabinet ministers often spoke in like vein. Yet Labour policy towards China was not simply founded upon ideals and notions of the world community. It was also based on an acknowledgement that in the field of world politics Asian nationalism was an increasingly potent force which it would be useful to harness, disastrous to thwart. The aim was therefore both to create or preserve favourable Anglo–Asian, and particularly Anglo–Indian relations, and to make it possible for the new China to avoid close dependence upon the Soviet Union.

Although Britain has managed to maintain reasonably good relations with neutralist Asia, Bevin's hopes of achieving a Sino–Western *détente* had small chance of realization. The halting of all rubber exports to China in May 1951, and Morrison's announcement the following month that no further efforts would be made to get Peking into the United Nations and that the question of Formosa was no longer of immediate concern, were an implicit recognition of this. Thus was Labour policy brought into line with Conservative. Indeed, responsible

[1] Peter Fleming, *The Sixth Column*, p. 60 (published 1951).

opinion in both parties had reached an approximate identity of view by the time the Far Eastern crisis was drawing to its close. On the Labour side there was a more realistic appreciation of Peking as a thoroughgoing Communist régime still in the throes of revolutionary zeal and dogmatism; amongst Conservatives was a greater awareness of the importance of Asian nationalism and of the need to consider the susceptibilities and probable reactions of the Asian Commonwealth countries, and of India especially.

Naturally, these divergencies from basic party attitudes were not achieved without strain. It was noticed that Tory back-benchers were much less enthusiastic than was the Labour Opposition about Eden's efforts to achieve a compromise peace in Indo-China. And without the responsibility of office, the Labour Party after 1951 was even more affected by those emotions and sentiments which are chiefly evinced on the back-benches or in the constituencies. In consequence the Labour leadership, to placate its Left-wing, had often to make a show of attacking the Government's policy or the Prime Minister's handling of affairs, but the issues were usually narrow and the displays of indignation exaggerated.

This is not to suggest that the views and proposals of the Labour Left lay entirely beyond the bounds of practical inter-national politics, although made up as it was of such diverse elements as neutralists, pacifists, and those admirers of the collectivist system who would never themselves submit to collectivist discipline, it is not easy to generalize. The source of the most vociferous and persistent criticisms of American policy, the dissenting Left was also a sounding-board for such anti-American sentiments as existed in Britain. This, together with the impression which arose that it found objectionable any measures taken by the West in its own defence, probably did something to obscure some of the sounder arguments pro-pounded from that quarter. One characteristic conclusion, shared by Bevan, the *New Statesman* and others, was that the West had become obsessed with the military threat of Com-munism, that it thereby risked losing the increasingly important economic and social struggle, and that as far as the under-developed parts of the world were concerned, the doctrine of containment which the Americans set such store by, was bound to prove fallacious. Although in general the Left has under-estimated the importance of military power, subsequent developments in Cuba, the Congo and South-East Asia have shown that this appraisal was not far wrong.

Despite their differences, or apparent differences, in periods of comparative calm, almost all sections of responsible political opinion in Britain were broadly of the same mind in times of major crisis. This was true over the outbreak of the Korean War when the resolve to counter aggression was almost unanimous. It was true also of those occasions when it seemed that American policy might lead to a full-scale war with China. The cry for caution and restraint which would then arise was partly the natural reaction of those regarding a great, and perhaps world, conflict as the ultimate disaster, but there were also more purely political reasons at work. Stability in the Far East best suited British interests. A war with China would cut off trade and imperil Hong Kong. It would also put an unbearable strain upon relations between Asia and the West. This in itself was sufficient to determine the Labour attitude. Moreover, with American attention and strength diverted to the Far East, Europe and the Middle East (both of much greater concern to Britain) would be left vulnerable to Soviet pressure—a consideration which weighed heavily, although not exclusively, with the Right. Indeed Churchill declared that nothing could be more foolish than for Western armies to be swallowed up in the vast spaces of China. Thus although Tory opinion tended to favour a policy of strength, it was strength without adventure. Unlike those of the Left, however, the comments of the Right upon American policies or pronouncements were invariably circumspect for fear of injuring a relationship of which it saw itself as the special guardian.

This British desire for stability was an important factor in the clash of British and American opinion over Far Eastern affairs. For a truly stable settlement is not one imposed and maintained by force, for the balance of forces may change, but an equitable arrangement in which dissatisfaction on both sides has been reduced to a minimum. Thus many in Britain were inclined to the view that in the resolving of outstanding issues, the Communists also should be given adequate satisfaction or guarantees. There was some demand for this at the close of the Korean War and a certain discontent with the Government's decision to subscribe to the Sixteen Nation Declaration of August 1953 which provided for retaliation if the Communists alone were responsible for breaking the truce.[1] Again, in June of the following year Eden proposed to the Americans that a Locarno type of settlement should be worked out for Indo-China, the idea being that certain powers should be asked to act as guarantors, and that if the fighting was resumed, these could take action against the aggressor without waiting for a unanimous agreement to do so.[2]

Such suggestions many Americans found either incomprehensible or repellent. Eden, in his *Memoirs*, records that his use of the word 'Locarno' raised a storm of outraged protest in the United States, and ascribes this to a confusion of the name in American minds with appeasement and Munich. The truth seems to have been, however, that American moral sentiment was scandalized at the prospect of a settlement which would involve reliance upon Communist good faith and guarantee Communist as well as anti-Communist territory.

Undoubtedly this fundamental difference of approach towards the threat of Communism in the Far East was largely owing to differences in the traditions and experiences of the British and American peoples. Indeed, it may even be argued that something of the sort was bound to arise between an old nation and one new to international responsibility. The Russo-Chinese disputes which first came into prominence in 1960 seem in part to be attributable to this cause. In both China and the United States bellicosity has been more marked than in Russia and Britain; and both (the United States more particularly under the Republicans who, to a greater degree than the Democrats, reflected the less mature, more chauvinistic side of American opinion) have dissented from their partners in holding that material aid should be given to their own declared supporters rather than to the uncommitted. These are interesting parallels, and in considering the explosive character of the Far

[1] Mainly, but not only, on the Left. See, for example: the *Observer*, leading article, 19 July 1953; *Tribune*, 13 August 1953; *Daily Herald*, leading article, 15 August 1953; *The Times*, letter from Gilbert Murray and other prominent figures in the United Nations Association, 21 August 1953.

[2] Eden, *Full Circle*, p. 133.

L

Eastern crisis, it is well to remember that the rival protagonists were powers in which two very different revolutionary traditions have survived most strongly.

Yet the Far East has for the Americans a strategical importance and a traditional attachment that it has never had for the British. And in recalling the excitability and stubbornness of American opinion as well as the legacy of American policy— the recurrently explosive situation in the Formosa Straits, the embarrassing impasse over the Chinese seat, the anti-American riots in South Korea and Japan, the military involvement in Vietnam—it is well to remember that in the Middle East British policy has not, since the war and taken as a whole, been conspicuously successful, nor has British opinion on the subject been remarkable for objectivity and restraint. Indeed, it can be argued that in each sphere the influence of that country which was the less emotionally or traditionally involved, helped to save the other from blunders and excesses which, even had they not led to a major conflict, would have done much to injure the reputation and weaken the influence of the Western democracies through large areas of the world.

APPENDIX I

Some Interest and Pressure Groups

THE CHINA ASSOCIATION

The China Association was founded in 1889 to protect and promote the interests of British firms trading with China, its functions being akin to those of a chamber of commerce. It keeps in close touch with the British Government and has access to the Chinese Government trade authorities.

The Association has a President (who from 1948 was Lord Inverchapel, and from 1950 Sir Horace Seymour, both former ambassadors to China), a Chairman, Vice-Chairman and General Committee of nineteen members. The Committee and officers are elected annually, almost all being representatives of firms and banks engaged in business with China. The Association, which is financed from the contributions and subscriptions of members, had a membership in 1949 of 197 firms and 230 individuals. Its head office is in the City of London.

At the time when the Communists were winning the civil war in China, the Association exerted its influence in favour of establishing good relations with them. In June 1949 it called the attention of publicists and M.P.s to certain bellicose British press statements and broadcasts which were causing concern amongst the British business community in China, and sought also to disabuse the Communists of any idea they may have gained that the reinforcement of Hong Kong signified a hostile attitude on the part of Great Britain. Again, later in the year the Association made strong representations to the British Government in favour of recognizing Communist China.

Once the Communists had established themselves and, from 1950, begun to subject British firms to pressures and exactions, the Association became intimately concerned in the difficult task of extricating the firms and their personnel from China and counselled the British Government accordingly.

During the Korean War the China Association sought to keep trade going in non-embargoed goods, it being able to maintain commercial relations with the Chinese Government even when British diplomatic contact with Peking had virtually ceased.

THE CHINA CAMPAIGN COMMITTEE

The China Campaign Committee was formed in 1937 following the Japanese invasion of China. Its object was to aid and publicize the Chinese cause in Britain and to foster Anglo-Chinese cultural relations.

Its founders and organizers included Dorothy Woodman, Secretary of the Union of Democratic Control, who remained its Honorary Secretary and moving spirit throughout; Victor Gollancz, the publisher; Margery Fry, the penal reformer; and Lord Listowel, who became the Committee's President. These were joined after the war by Mrs. (later Lady) Selwyn-Clarke, who until her internment by the Japanese had handled the Chinese end of the Committee's activities, and by Michael (later Lord) Lindsay. Both had become acquainted with leading Chinese personalities, Nationalist and Communist, during their years in China.

Until the close of the Second World War, the Committee, which had earlier campaigned for the reopening of the Burma Road,[1] had co-operated equally with the Kuomintang and Communist authorities, although it was always more difficult to send money and medical supplies to Yenan than to Chungking. With, however, the relapse of China into civil war, it came increasingly to support the cause of the Communists, a policy which reflected the views and sentiments of its mainly Left-wing membership as well as the growing disgust of its Sinophile element for the Kuomintang.

Following the victory of Chinese Communism in 1949, the Honorary Secretary resisted a Communist move to turn the organization into a fully committed supporter of the new régime, and the China Campaign Committee was allowed to lapse.

THE BRITAIN–CHINA FRIENDSHIP ASSOCIATION

This was a Communist front organization set up shortly after the establishment of Communist China. It aimed to promote a favourable image of the new régime in Britain, and to this end organized meetings and arranged visits. Its President was the eminent Sinologist Dr. Joseph Needham, who in 1952 supported the Chinese

[1] This last remaining supply route into China was, under Japanese pressure, temporarily closed by the British Government in the summer of 1940. The China Campaign Committee thereupon organized in Britain a petition to get it reopened which was signed by, or on behalf of, a million supporters.

charges of germ warfare in a lengthy report. The Secretary of the Association was J. Dribbon. There was no journal.

In 1950 it sponsored the visit to Britain of the Liu Ning-i 'friendship delegation' which studiously insulted almost all its hosts from the Labour Party Executive to the Lord Mayor of Manchester.[1]

In 1951 the B.C.F.A. attempted to join forces with the Peace with China Council (see Appendix II) but was rebuffed.

[1] Michael Lindsay, *China and the Cold War*, pp. 12–16.

APPENDIX II

The Peace with China Movement

THE NATIONAL PEACE COUNCIL

The first steps in organizing public action over the danger of war in the Far East were taken by the National Peace Council. This is an independent body, founded in 1908, and not committed to any one political view or movement, or even to pacifism. In 1950 the President of the N.P.C. was Lord Boyd-Orr, former Director-General of the Food and Agriculture Organization, who had been awarded the Nobel Peace Prize the previous year. Its Chairman was the Rev. Henry Carter, a prominent Methodist, who, upon his death in June 1951, was succeeded by Reginald Sorensen, M.P. The work of the N.P.C. largely lay in co-ordinating the activities of many different bodies and individuals having a common interest in peace. It was not associated with Communist peace organizations.

Four days after the outbreak of war in Korea, the N.P.C. addressed an appeal to the Soviet, British and American Governments to use their influence to stop the fighting. Nearly a month later, on 24 July 1950, the first public meeting on Korea was held in the Kingsway Hall, speakers from the three main parties again making this appeal as well as urging the admission of Peking to the United Nations. The next meeting did not take place until 27 November when, following the Chinese intervention in Korea, Kingsley Martin, Tom Driberg, M.P., who had just returned from Korea, and others addressed a packed gathering.[1] The object was to encourage Attlee and Bevin to take a firmer line over MacArthur, but the meeting was virtually ignored by the national press.

The third Kingsway Hall meeting was held on 8 January 1951. The chairman was Lord Stansgate and the speakers were Norman Bower, M.P., Michael Foot, M.P., Reginald Sorensen, M.P., Ritchie Calder, the Rev. Henry Carter, and Kingsley Martin. The Leader of the Parliamentary Liberal Party, Clement Davies, was also advertised to speak, but being unable to attend, sent a message. The American proposal, then before the United Nations, to condemn Communist China as an aggressor and afterwards apply sanctions, was strongly attacked. The hall on this occasion was packed,

[1] National Peace Council, *Annual Report, 1951.*

many being unable to gain admission even to the large overflow
meeting.[1]

THE PEACE WITH CHINA COUNCIL

In view of the widespread concern about events in the Far East, the
N.P.C. decided to sponsor a separate body, to be known as the
Peace with China Council, which, at least to begin with, it would
provide with facilities and funds. Kingsley Martin announced the
formation of this body at the Kingsway Hall meeting of 8 January,
calling at the same time for the setting up of local committees
throughout the country. The national Council consisted chiefly of
interested public figures living in the London area. These included:

Lady Archibald, former Labour L.C.C. councillor.
Norman Bower, Conservative M.P.
Ritchie Calder, editorial staff, *New Statesman* and science editor,
    News Chronicle (later Labour peer).
Rev. Henry Carter, Chairman N.P.C.
Donald Chesworth, future Labour L.C.C. councillor.
Lord Chorley, Labour peer and lawyer.
Desmond Donnelly, Labour M.P.
Tom Driberg, Labour M.P.
David Ennals, Secretary U.N. Association and Liberal parlia-
    mentary candidate (later Labour M.P.).
Lord Faringdon, Labour peer.
Norman MacKenzie, editorial staff, *New Statesman*.
Kingsley Martin, editor, *New Statesman*.
John Mendelson, future Labour M.P.
Lady Selwyn-Clarke, future Labour L.C.C. councillor.
Leslie G. D. Smith, Director N.P.C.
Reginald Sorensen, Labour M.P.
Lord Stansgate, Labour peer.
Miss Dorothy Woodman, Hon. Secretary late China Campaign
    Committee.

An executive committee was set up of which Lord Chorley became
chairman. Soon sufficient money was being collected and donated
for the Council to invite Donald Chesworth to act as paid secretary.

Much was made of Norman Bower's membership in order to
overcome the suspicion, prevalent at the time, that all peace movements were either Communist or fellow-travelling. Moreover,
Communist requests to participate were refused and Communists
were discouraged from infiltrating by the stress laid upon the fact of

[1] Ibid.

North Korean aggression. Nevertheless the movement attracted small support on the Right, remaining predominantly radical and receiving little press publicity except in the *New Statesman*.

The policy of the campaign was set out in a leaflet, published in January 1951, entitled *The Peril of World War*. In this the Peace with China Council expressed grave misgiving about MacArthur's political conduct and military judgement, and although supporting the original United Nations action against North Korea, declared that the crisis had arisen from many causes of which Korea was only one. Five principles were then listed:

1. That the Cairo and Potsdam decisions on Formosa were binding on the signatories.
2. That Britain, in concert with the Commonwealth and other United Nations members, should press for the admission of Communist China to the Security Council.
3. That there should be no extension of the Korean conflict.
4. That there should be an early and equitable settlement in Korea and the creation, in accordance with United Nations intentions, of a united, independent state.
5. That Britain should co-operate fully with India, Pakistan and other Asian countries in getting the United Nations to solve outstanding political problems and to plan the economic rehabilitation of Korea.

Finally an appeal was made for the formation of local committees. Some 60,000 copies of this leaflet were distributed.

Meanwhile the movement was gathering way in other parts of the country. Local committees were soon organized and meetings arranged at Manchester, Reading, Lewisham, Chelsea, Bow, and many other places in London and the provinces. The Glasgow branch was particularly strong. The central office received innumerable requests for help and guidance, and was largely responsible for providing speakers for some 200 meetings held throughout the country during the first three months of the campaign.

The story of the Hampstead Peace with China Council may be cited to show how one of these local movements was set up and how it operated. As early as 5 January 1951 there was correspondence in the local press supporting the views of the Archbishop of York, Lord Silkin, and others, that efforts should be made to stop the drift to war. By 26 January a Peace with China Council had been formed by a few Hampstead Socialists. The first large meeting was held in the Town Hall on 5 February, invitations to attend being issued to the three main parties, the churches, the British Legion and other organizations. The speakers included Sydney Silverman, M.P.,

Geoffrey Bing, M.P., Kingsley Martin, and a Lt.-Col. Nicholas Read-Collins who brought an authoritative touch to the proceedings through having served on MacArthur's staff in Japan. At the close of the meeting a resolution was passed which reiterated the view that Formosa and the Chinese seat should be given to Peking, and which expressed disappointment that the Government had supported the American move in the United Nations to condemn China as an aggressor. Finally, after a collection had obtained £70 for campaign expenses, some 800 prepared postcards declaring that the Prime Minister would have the backing of the nation if he insisted that Britain would not take part in a war against China, were distributed for signing and posting to Downing Street. The success of this meeting led to inquiries from other boroughs by those wishing to organize similar campaigns, as well as to plans to call a conference of all the Peace with China Councils in North and North West London. Later in the month, on 24 February, another meeting was held and was addressed by Sir John Pratt, Margery Fry, and F. Elwyn Jones, M.P.—the first causing the organizers much embarrassment by maintaining that it was South Korea which had attacked the North. After this a newsletter was started, and Hampstead sent five delegates to a national conference of the whole movement held in London on 15 July 1951.

However, after MacArthur's dismissal in April 1951, the Peace with China campaign lost much of its impetus, and with the opening of truce negotiations in July, there seemed little possibility that Korea would again become a major threat to world peace. In consequence the Council met less frequently, fewer public meetings were organized, and the luxury of a paid secretary was dispensed with. Lord Chorley gave up the chairmanship of the executive committee, and neither he nor Donald Chesworth, the secretary, could recollect in later years that the Peace with China Council had survived their departure.

In fact the Council continued to function, although at a steadier tempo, for another two years. Reginald Sorensen became chairman of the executive committee, and Mrs. Joan Mineau, a founder of the Hampstead branch and a Fabian, took over the work of organizing and brought order to the finances. In September 1951 the Council condemned the Japanese peace treaty on the grounds that it ignored China, offended neutralist Asia and ensured that Japan should be an American base.[1] On 4 March 1952 it held a public meeting in the Central Hall, Westminster, which was attended by some 2,000 people. One of the speakers was Kenneth Younger, M.P.,

---

[1] *Manchester Guardian*, 20 September 1951.

who declared that it was vital the Chinese should know that the
United Nations were not concerned to undo their revolution.[1]
Others who spoke were Ritchie Calder, James Cameron (a former
war correspondent in Korea), Kingsley Martin and Mrs. Barbara
Castle, M.P.[2]

The *début* of Eisenhower and Dulles on the international stage
resulted in one last burst of activity. A mass meeting was held in the
Kingsway Hall on 2 March 1953 primarily to protest against the
new President's decision to make the Seventh Fleet the guardian not
of Formosa and the mainland impartially, but of the island alone.
Lord Stansgate again took the chair, the speakers being Sir Compton
Mackenzie, R. H. S. Crossman, M.P., Dr. Donald Soper, Kingsley
Martin, Emrys Hughes, M.P., K. Shelvankar of India, and Fareed
Jafri of Pakistan.[3] A second meeting soon followed on 1 April at the
Central Hall, Westminster. Here the chief speaker was Aneurin
Bevan, who had just returned from a visit to India and Pakistan. He
declared that the necessary condition for peace in the Far East was
the immediate disbanding of the Nationalist army in Formosa.[4]
These two meetings brought some £300 to the Peace with China
campaign fund. At the same time the Council published a pamphlet
in which Desmond Donnelly attacked the Dulles doctrine of liberation or 'roll back'. The Sixteen Nation Declaration and Dulles's
support for Syngman Rhee at the time of the Korean armistice were
also condemned in a memorandum issued by the Council on 12
August.

With the end of the war in Korea it seemed that the work of the
Peace with China Council was over. In August 1953 it was therefore
adjourned indefinitely, its members intending to meet again if the
situation should become sufficiently dangerous. However, neither
the Indo-China crisis of the following spring, nor the later troubles
over the off-shore islands in the Formosa Straits, led to its resurrec-
tion.

What was the essential character of the movement, and what influence did it have? In many ways it was a typical product of the
idealistic and Left-wing elements of British radicalism, its speakers
and organizers tending to be either well-known philanthropist-
reformers, like Sylvia Pankhurst, Lady Parmoor, and Margery Fry,
or such luminaries of the Left as Sydney Silverman, R. H. S. Cross-

---

[1] Ibid., 5 March 1952.

[2] National Peace Council, *Annual Report, 1952.*

[3] National Peace Council, *Annual Report, 1953*; *Manchester Guardian* and
News Chronicle, 3 March 1953.

[4] *Manchester Guardian*, 2 April 1953.

man and A. J. P. Taylor. Not surprisingly, many of those who were active in the Peace with China movement later took a leading part in the Campaign for Nuclear Disarmament. Yet for a short time it was something more: the almost spontaneous expression of a deep and widespread concern amongst ordinary people that the United States, with Britain in tow, might recklessly involve at least half the world in war. This was noticed by the organizers and by journalists, who were frequently struck by the size and seriousness of the meetings. Even more than the letters to the national press or the intensive lobbying of M.P.s—an effective part of the Council's work—the rapid growth and spontaneity of the movement in the months preceding MacArthur's recall must have indicated to official and foreign opinion alike how the temper and judgement of a great part of the country stood in these matters.[1]

[1] The major Peace with China Council meetings were attended by American Embassy officials.

APPENDIX III

Public Opinion Polls

Section A The Recognition Question

,,   *B* The Chinese Seat

,,   *C* Formosa

,,   *D* Korea

,,   *E* Indo-China and Geneva

,,   *F* Anglo-American Relations

Details of the following polls have been included by courtesy of Social Surveys (Gallup Poll) Ltd. from whose records they have been taken.

All figures given are percentages.

Section A The Recognition Question

A 1. Date of Poll: 28 November 1949

QUESTION: *Do you think that Britain should recognize the Government set up in China by the Chinese Communist Party, that is, should we send an ambassador and have dealings with this Communist Government?*

	YES	NO	DON'T KNOW
Total	29	45	26
Voting intention			
Conservative	23	59	18
Labour	34	37	29
Liberal	37	37	26

A 2. 4 October 1950

Have you heard or read about the situation in Formosa? Of those who had—Do you agree or disagree with Britain's continuing to recognize the Chinese Communist Government?

	AGREE	DISAGREE	DON'T KNOW
Total	27	20	12
Conservative	17	33	14
Labour	36	11	10
Liberal	31	17	13

NOTE: The purpose of the prefatory question is not clear. The object may have been to test the reactions of those who were aware that the Nationalists now had a good prospect of survival.   B.E.P.

A 3. 20 February 1951

Which do you think we should do, continue to recognize the Communist Government in China, or should we stop our recognition?

	CONTINUE	STOP	DON'T KNOW
Total	41	34	25
Conservative	33	45	22
Labour	51	24	25
Liberal	52	26	22

Section B The Chinese Seat

B 1. 20 February 1951

Do you think we should continue to support the admission of Communist China into the United Nations, or should we oppose her admission?

	SUPPORT	OPPOSE	DON'T KNOW
Total	40	35	25
Conservative	32	47	21
Labour	50	25	25
Liberal	44	29	27

NOTE: This was the earliest poll taken in Britain on the subject of the Chinese seat. Even before the Korean War, American opinion presented a striking contrast: 'Do you think that Communist China should or should not be admitted as a member of the United Nations?' Should—11; Should not—58; Don't know—31 (poll taken in U.S., early or mid-June 1950).

B 2. 15–17 May 1953

If there is an end to the fighting in Korea, do you think that the United Nations should or should not admit Communist China as a member?

	SHOULD	SHOULD NOT	DON'T KNOW
Total	43	36	21
Conservative	36	48	16
Labour	48	31	21
Liberal	53	22	25

NOTE: This poll may be compared with one taken in the United States in July 1953: 'Would you approve or disapprove of giving the Chinese Communists a seat on the United Nations Security Council if the Communists agree to peace terms in Korea?' Approve—23; Disapprove—60; Don't know—17.

B 3. 12–24 June 1953

Do you think that China should or should not be admitted as a member of the United Nations?

	SHOULD	SHOULD NOT	DON'T KNOW
Total	52	21	27

B 4. 5–15 September 1953

If there is a settlement in Korea, do you think that the United Nations should or should not admit the Chinese People's Republic as a member?

	SHOULD	SHOULD NOT	DON'T KNOW
Total	57	16	27
Conservative	52	21	27
Labour	63	13	24
Liberal	59	11	30

NOTE: This poll may be compared with one taken at the same time in the United States: 'If the Chinese Communists agree to withdraw all their troops from Korea, would you approve or disapprove of giving the Chinese Communists a seat on the United Nations Security Council?' Approve—21; Disapprove—68; Don't know—11.

B 5. 20–31 March 1954

Do you think that Communist China should or should not be admitted as a member of the United Nations?

	SHOULD	SHOULD NOT	DON'T KNOW
Total	45	17	38

B 6. 25–27 June 1954

Mr. Attlee says that the failure to admit the Chinese People's Republic to the United Nations is a major obstacle to agreement in the Far East. Would you approve or disapprove if China were admitted as a member of the United Nations?

	APPROVE	DISAPPROVE	DON'T KNOW
Total	61	20	19
Conservative	56	23	21
Labour	69	17	14
Liberal	66	20	14

NOTE: This poll may be compared with one taken in the United States in July 1954: 'Do you think Communist China should or should not be admitted as a member of the United Nations?' Should—7; Should not—78; Don't know—15. Dr. Gallup commented (24 July 1954): 'In the nearly 20 years that the Gallup Poll has been sampling public opinion in Great Britain and the United States, there never has been an issue over which the people of the two countries are so far apart in their thinking as they are on the controversial question of admitting Communist China to the United Nations.' In August 1954, a further American poll put the question: 'Suppose a majority of the other members of the United Nations votes to admit Communist China. Do you think the United States should resign its membership in the United Nations or not?' Should—25; Should not—59; Don't know—16.

B 7. 29–31 January 1955

Do you think that arrangements should or should not be made for admitting the Peking Government as a member of the United Nations?

	SHOULD	SHOULD NOT	DON'T KNOW
Total	59	20	21
Conservative	57	25	18
Labour	63	16	21
Liberal	65	16	19

Section C Formosa

C 1. 29–31 January 1955
If the United States gets involved in fighting in Formosa, should we join in on her side or stay out?

	JOIN IN	STAY OUT	DON'T KNOW
Total	20	65	15
Conservative	28	58	14
Labour	14	75	11
Liberal	19	67	14

NOTE: These three polls have been included because, although later than the period of this study, they were the first to be taken in Britain on the subject of Formosa. B.E.P.

C 2. Taken with C 1.
Do you think that the United States is right or wrong to defend Chiang Kai-shek in Formosa?

	RIGHT	WRONG	DON'T KNOW
Total	31	43	26
Conservative	43	35	22
Labour	24	52	24
Liberal	26	45	29

C 3. Taken with C 1.
What do you think is the best thing to do about Formosa?
   (a) Leave it with Chiang Kai-shek and defend him there?
   (b) Allow control to pass to the Peking Government?
   (c) Give control of it to the United Nations?

	(a)	*(b)*	*(c)*	DON'T KNOW
Total	15	10	56	19
Conservative	18	5	64	13
Labour	12	15	54	19
Liberal	12	13	59	16

Section D Korea

D 1. 3 July 1950

Have you heard about the fighting in Korea? Of those who had—Do you approve or disapprove of the action that has been taken by the British and American Governments?

	APPROVE	DISAPPROVE	DON'T KNOW
Total	69	14	15
Conservative	80	7	11
Labour	63	18	17
Liberal	72	7	20

D 2. 4 October 1950

Do you approve or disapprove of sending British troops to fight in Korea?

	APPROVE	DISAPPROVE	DON'T KNOW
Total	63	31	6
Conservative	73	22	5
Labour	58	35	7
Liberal	62	31	7

D 3. Taken with D 2.

What is your main feeling about the situation in Korea: the fighting should go on until the North Koreans are beaten, or should the United Nations try to negotiate a settlement?

	NORTH KOREANS BEATEN	U.N. SETTLEMENT	DON'T KNOW
Total	50	41	9
Conservative	63	29	8
Labour	43	47	10
Liberal	43	51	6

M

D 4. Taken with D 2.

Do you think that the fighting in Korea will lead to a third world war?

	YES	NO	DON'T KNOW
Total	14	57	29
Conservative	14	60	26
Labour	14	56	30
Liberal	10	56	34

D 5. January 1951

Would you say there is much danger of world war or not much danger?

	MUCH DANGER	NOT MUCH DANGER	DON'T KNOW
Total	58	29	13
Conservative	56	33	11
Labour	62	25	13

D 6. Taken with D 5.

What do you think we should do in Korea?

   (1) *Stop the fighting:* total 47.
      (a) *Get out; withdraw.*
      (b) *Negotiate; 4-Power conference.*
      (c) *Try and save what we can.*

	(a)	(b)	(c)
Total	30	15	2
Conservative	22	17	2
Labour	29	16	3

   (2) *Carry on fighting:* total 26.
      (a) *Show our strength; hold our ground.*
      (b) *Fight it out; smash the Reds.*
      (c) *Fight back to the 38th Parallel.*
      (d) *Use the A-bomb.*

	(a)	(b)	(c)	(d)
Total	18	4	3	1
Conservative	25	4	4	3
Labour	16	5	3	0

(3) *Other replies:* total 7.

(4) *Don't know:* total 20.

NOTE: The slight discrepancy between some of the party figures and the totals may be accounted for by the omission of the Liberal figures.   B.E.P.

D 7. Taken with D 5.

Do you think that General MacArthur is doing a good job or a bad job in Korea?

	GOOD	BAD	DON'T KNOW
Total	28	40	32
Conservative	39	29	32
Labour	23	47	30

D 8. 20 February 1951

Should the United Nations get out of Korea, or, if they reach the 38th Parallel, should they stay there and negotiate, or should they continue to advance beyond the 38th?

	GET OUT	NEGO-TIATE	ADVANCE	DON'T KNOW
Total	14	53	17	16
Conservative	8	55	21	16
Labour	18	52	14	16
Liberal	13	61	13	13

D 9. 9 May 1951

Do you approve or disapprove of President Truman's having dismissed General MacArthur?

	APPROVE	DISAPPROVE	DON'T KNOW
Total	55	19	26
Conservative	49	25	26
Labour	65	14	21
Liberal	59	13	28

NOTE: The American figures for this question were: Approve—25; Disapprove—66; Don't know—9. (May 1951)

D 10. Taken with D 9.

What do you think is the best thing to do about the fighting in Korea, keep it in Korea only or extend it into China as well?

	KOREA ONLY	CHINA AS WELL	DON'T KNOW
Total	72	10	18
Conservative	69	14	17
Labour	79	7	14
Liberal	73	9	18

NOTE: This poll may be compared with one taken in the United States in February 1951: 'Do you think the United States should start an all out war with Communist China or not?' Should start war—14; Should not—77; Don't know—9.

D 11. 2 August 1951

Do you think it was a good idea or a poor idea for the United Nations to agree to peace talks in Korea?

	GOOD	POOR	DON'T KNOW
Total	82	8	10
Conservative	78	12	10
Labour	86	5	9
Liberal	85	9	6

D 12. Taken with D 11.

Taking everything into account, which side do you think will have come off best if the war in Korea ends with Korea still divided at the 38th Parallel?

	U.N.	COMMUNISTS	NEITHER	DON'T KNOW
Total	17	18	30	35
Conservative	17	23	30	30
Labour	20	14	30	36
Liberal	15	17	32	36

D 13. 22 December 1952.

Which of these do you think the United Nations should do in the war in Korea?

 (a) Negotiate peace whilst maintaining present battle line?

 (b) Pull out of Korea?

 (c) Continue a 'limited war' using South Koreans as far as possible?

 (d) All out war against China and North Korea, to drive to the Manchurian border?

	(a)	*(b)*	*(c)*	*(d)*	DON'T KNOW
Total	43	17	10	8	22
Conservative	48	10	12	11	19
Labour	40	26	7	7	20
Liberal	47	15	17	8	13

D 14. 3–15 March 1953

Do you agree or disagree with the idea of blockading China?

	AGREE	DISAGREE	DON'T KNOW
Total	15	37	48
Conservative	22	34	44
Labour	9	43	48
Liberal	20	41	39

D 15. 7–10 May 1953

Do you approve or disapprove of the way the truce negotiations in Korea are being handled by the United Nations representatives?

	APPROVE	DISAPPROVE	DON'T KNOW
Total	31	37	32
Conservative	41	29	30
Labour	25	45	30
Liberal	32	32	36

D 16. 15–17 May 1953

At present the Americans are acting as spokesmen for the United Nations in the Korea truce negotiations. Should it be left this way or should other nations join in?

	LEFT THIS WAY	OTHERS JOIN IN	DON'T KNOW
Total	13	77	10
Conservative	21	73	6
Labour	7	83	10
Liberal	12	75	13

D 17. 31 July–13 August 1953

Do you approve or disapprove of the terms of the armistice in Korea?

	APPROVE	DISAPPROVE	DON'T KNOW
Total	50	10	40

D 18. 11–20 December 1953

Do you think it is likely or unlikely that there will be further fighting in Korea?

	LIKELY	UNLIKELY	DON'T KNOW
Total	22	44	34

D 19. Taken with D 18

If the Communists start fighting again, do you think that we should continue to help the South Koreans?

	SHOULD	SHOULD NOT	DON'T KNOW
Total	43	31	26

D 20. Taken with D 18

If the South Koreans start fighting again, do you think that we should continue to help them?

	SHOULD	SHOULD NOT	DON'T KNOW
Total	16	57	27

NOTE: The American figures for this question were: for sending U.S. soldiers; Should—31; Should not—56; Don't know—13; for sending war material, Should—63; Should not—27; Don't know—10. (December 1953).

D 21. Taken with D 18

Do you think that the United Nations should try to unify Korea or leave the situation as it is, with the North Koreans at the truce line?

	TRY TO UNIFY	LEAVE	DON'T KNOW
Total	40	36	24

Section E Indo-China and Geneva

E 1. 20–31 March 1954

Next month Great Britain, America, Russia, Communist China and France are meeting at Geneva to discuss Far Eastern problems. Do you think this meeting is a good thing or a bad thing?

	GOOD	BAD	DON'T KNOW
Total	71	4	25

E 2. Taken with E 1

Do you think that this meeting is or is not likely to improve relations between the Big Powers?

	IS	IS NOT	DON'T KNOW
Total	43	33	24

E 3. 23–25 April 1954

Mr. Dulles (the American Foreign Secretary) has proposed that we should join in with other countries to stop further advances of Communism in the Far East. Mr. Eden says that Britain will give very serious consideration to the proposal. What are your views?

    (a) We should do all we can to support Mr. Dulles?

    (b) We should support him only if countries like India join in with us?

    (c) We should do all we can at Geneva and afterwards to reach agreement with China before considering the Dulles plan?

    (d) We should have nothing to do with the Dulles plan?

	(a)	(b)	(c)	(d)	DON'T KNOW
Total	31	15	31	10	13
Conservative	42	13	29	6	10
Labour	21	17	34	15	13
Liberal	32	17	35	8	8

E 4. 19 May–2 June 1954

Would you approve or disapprove of sending soldiers to take part in the fighting in Indo-China?

	APPROVE	DISAPPROVE	DON'T KNOW
Total	10	73	17

NOTE: The American figures for this question were: Approve—22; Disapprove—68; Don't know—10. (May 1954)

E 5. Taken with E 4

Would you approve or disapprove of our sending air and naval forces, but not ground forces, to help the French?

	APPROVE	DISAPPROVE	DON'T KNOW
Total	17	63	20

NOTE: The American figures for this question were: Approve—36; Disapprove—52; Don't know—12. (May 1954)

E 6. 25–27 June 1954

Do you think that the discussions on Indo-China and Far Eastern problems now taking place in Geneva have decreased or increased world tension or left things much as they were?

	DE-CREASED	IN-CREASED	AS THEY WERE	DON'T KNOW
Total	16	22	45	17
Conservative	17	22	46	15
Labour	15	22	44	19
Liberal	17	24	53	6

E 7. Taken with E 6

Are you in favour of continuing with them or do you think we should withdraw from the Conference?

	CONTINUE	WITHDRAW	DON'T KNOW
Total	67	14	19
Conservative	72	12	16
Labour	64	17	19
Liberal	67	16	17

E 8. Taken with E 6

What are your views on the suggestion that Britain joins with America, France and the non-Communist nations of Asia in an Eastern Security Pact?
   (a) We should join regardless of events at Geneva?
   (b) We should join only if the Geneva Conference fails?
   (c) We should not join on any account?

	(a)	*(b)*	*(c)*	DON'T KNOW
Total	38	20	16	26
Conservative	43	20	12	25
Labour	32	19	23	26
Liberal	36	29	10	25

Of those answering *(a)* or *(b)*:

If some of the free Asian countries refuse to join such a pact, should we or should we not go ahead without them?

	SHOULD	SHOULD NOT	DON'T KNOW
Total	44	8	6
Conservative	51	9	3
Labour	39	6	6
Liberal	51	10	4

Section F Anglo-American Relations

F 1. January 1951

Should a war come do you think it is likely to arise through America, Russia, or some other way?

	AMERICA	RUSSIA	BOTH	OTHER WAY	DON'T KNOW
Total	21	58	6	6	9
Conservative	8	78	3	8	3
Labour	25	51	8	6	10

F 2. Taken with F 1

Which of these statements do you agree with most on relations between America and ourselves?

(a) We are natural allies and should always stick together?

(b) We should act together on most things but Britain should remain independent?

(c) We can act together where our policy is the same, but otherwise Britain should remain independent?

(d) Our relations should be on the same footing as with other countries?

	(a)	*(b)*	*(c)*	*(d)*	DON'T KNOW
Total	22	29	23	21	5
Conservative	34	33	20	7	6
Labour	16	28	23	29	4

F 3. 20 February 1951

Do you approve or disapprove of the role that America is playing in world affairs?

	APPROVE	DISAPPROVE	DON'T KNOW
Total	40	35	25
Conservative	53	27	20
Labour	27	45	28
Liberal	41	34	25

F 4. 18–26 March 1952

Do you approve or disapprove of the role that America is playing in world affairs?

	APPROVE	DISAPPROVE	DON'T KNOW
Total	37	34	29

F 5. 23–25 April 1954

Do you approve or disapprove of the role the United States is now playing in world affairs?

	APPROVE	DISAPPROVE	DON'T KNOW
Total	37	40	23
Conservative	55	26	19
Labour	24	54	22
Liberal	39	36	25

F 6. Taken with F 5

Some people say that we are giving in too much to the United States in our foreign policy. Do you agree or disagree?

	AGREE	DISAGREE	DON'T KNOW
Total	56	31	13
Conservative	43	46	11
Labour	71	18	11
Liberal	53	33	14

Bibliography

NOTE: The bibliography is divided into two parts. The first contains works treating of British opinion or policy together with those which may be taken as contemporary expressions of British opinion for the period 1945–54. The second part consists of a selection of works covering various aspects of the Far Eastern Crisis of 1945–54. The place of publication is London unless otherwise indicated.

BRITISH OPINION AND POLICY

OFFICIAL PUBLICATIONS

Parliamentary Debates (Hansard):

House of Commons Debates, 5th Series
House of Lords Debates, 5th Series

Command Papers on the Korean War:

Summary of Events, 1950: Cmd. 8078 (1950).
U.N. Resolution on Chinese Intervention: Cmd. 8159 (1951).
Further Summary of Events, October 1950–May 1951: Cmd. 8366 (1951).
Armistice Negotiations and Prisoner of War Camps, June 1951– May 1952: Cmd. 8596 (1952).
Indian Proposal for Resolving the Prisoners of War Problem: Cmd. 8716 (1952).
Further Developments to January 1953: Cmd. 8793 (1953).
Armistice Agreement at Panmunjom: Cmd. 8938 (1953).

Miscellaneous Command Papers:

The Prime Minister's Visit to the United States: Cmd. 8110 (1950).
Correspondence between the British and Chinese Governments on British Trade in China: Cmd. 8639 (1952).
British Involvement in the Indo-China Conflict 1945-65 (Documents): Cmnd. 2834 (1965).
The Geneva Conference (Documents): Cmd. 9186 and Cmd. 9239 (1954).

CHRONICLES AND DOCUMENTS

Survey of International Affairs. R.I.I.A.
Documents on International Affairs. R.I.I.A.
British Foreign Policy: Some Relevant Documents, January 1950– April 1955. R.I.I.A., 1955.
Annual Register. Longmans.

BOOKS

ALLEN, H. C., *Great Britain and the United States* (chap. 19). Odhams, 1954.

ATTLEE, C. R., *As it Happened*. Heinemann, 1954.

EDEN, SIR ANTHONY, *Memoirs: Full Circle*. Cassell, 1960.

EPSTEIN, LEON D., *Britain—Uneasy Ally*. University of Chicago Press, 1955.

GOODWIN, GEOFFREY L., *Britain and the United Nations*. Oxford University Press, 1957.

HUDSON, G. F., *Questions of East and West*. Odhams, 1953.

INGRAM, KENNETH, *History of the Cold War*. Finlayson, 1955.

LINDSAY, MICHAEL, *China and the Cold War*. Melbourne University Press, 1955.

LUARD, EVAN, *Britain and China*. Chatto and Windus, 1962.

McKITTERICK, T. E. M. and KENNETH YOUNGER, *Fabian International Essays* (chap. V, The Far East by Kenneth Younger). Hogarth Press, 1957.

MORAN LORD, *Winston Churchill: The Struggle for Survival, 1940–1965*. Constable, 1966.

MORRISON OF LAMBETH, LORD, *Herbert Morrison: An Autobiography*. Odhams, 1960.

NICHOLAS, H. G., *Britain and the United States*. Chatto and Windus, 1963.

NORTHEDGE, F. S., *British Foreign Policy: The Process of Readjustment 1945–1961*. Allen and Unwin, 1962.

OLVER, A. S. B., *Outline of British Policy in East and South-East Asia, 1945–May 1950*. R.I.I.A., 1950.

PELLING, H. M., *America and the British Left: from Bright to Bevan*. Black, 1956.

PRITT, D. N., S. O. DAVIES, R. PALME DUTT, etc., *Korea Handbook*. A *Labour Monthly* publication, 1950.

ROBERTS, HENRY L. and PAUL A. WILSON, *Britain and the United States: Problems in Co-operation*. R.I.I.A., 1953.

VAN DER SPRENKEL, OTTO B., MICHAEL LINDSAY and ROBERT GUILLAIN, *New China: Three Views*. Turnstile Press, 1950.

WILLIAMS, FRANCIS, *A Prime Minister Remembers*. Heinemann, 1961.

WINDRICH, ELAINE, *British Labour's Foreign Policy*. Stanford University Press, 1952.

WOODHOUSE, C. M., *British Foreign Policy since the Second World War*. Hutchinson, 1961.

YOUNGER, KENNETH, *Three Public Addresses: Some New Factors in Post-War British Foreign Policy. Britain and the Far East. Britain and the Commonwealth.* (Dyason Lectures, 1955.) Melbourne, Australian Institute of International Affairs, 1955.

PAMPHLETS

CROSSMAN, R. H. S. and KENNETH YOUNGER, *Socialist Foreign Policy.* Fabian International Bureau, Tract 287, April 1951.

DONNELLY, DESMOND, *Speak for Britain*: *No War with China.* Peace with China Council pamphlet, March 1953.

MACKENZIE, NORMAN, *Conspiracy for War: The China Lobby.* Union of Democratic Control pamphlet, 1952.

PRATT, SIR JOHN, *Korea: the Lie that led to War.* Britain-China Friendship Association pamphlet, 1951.

PRITT, D. N., *New Light on Korea.* A *Labour Monthly* pamphlet, 1951 Series: No. 5.

PURCELL, VICTOR, *War or Settlement in the Far East?* Peace Aims Pamphlet 53, National Peace Council, March 1952.

READ-COLLINS, NICHOLAS, *Report on the War in Indo-China.* Union of Democratic Control pamphlet, October 1953.

TOWNSEND, PETER, *In China Now.* Union of Democratic Control pamphlet, 1953.

ARTICLES

AMERY, JULIAN, 'The Inexcusable War', *Nineteenth Century and After,* January 1950.

ATTLEE, C. R., 'Britain and America: Common Aims, Different Opinions', *Foreign Affairs,* January 1954.

COLLAR, H. J., 'British Commercial Relations with China', *International Affairs,* October 1953.

EPSTEIN, LEON D., 'The British Labour Left and U.S. Foreign Policy', *American Political Science Review,* December 1951.

FITZMAURICE, G. G., 'Chinese Representation in the United Nations', *Year Book of World Affairs,* 1952.

GAITSKELL, HUGH, 'The Search for Anglo-American Policy', *Foreign Affairs,* July 1954.

GHERSON, RANDOLPH, 'British Recognition of China: Some Issues Examined', *New Commonwealth,* March 1950.

GOOLD-ADAMS, R., 'Formosa—The British View', *English-Speaking World,* March 1955.

HAFFNER, SEBASTIAN, 'The Anglo-American Quarrel: Another View', *Twentieth Century,* October 1953.

HUDSON, G. F., 'Privileged Sanctuary', *Twentieth Century*, January 1951.

HUDSON, G. F., 'Will Britain and America Split in Asia?', *Foreign Affairs*, July 1953.

HUDSON, G. F., 'The Anglo-American Quarrel', *Twentieth Century*, October 1953.

HUDSON, G. F., 'The Problem of China', *United Empire*, May–June 1954.

MAKINS, SIR ROGER, 'The World since the War: The Third Phase', *Foreign Affairs*, October 1954.

YOUNGER, KENNETH, 'Public Opinion and Foreign Policy', *British Journal of Sociology*, June 1955.

THE FAR EASTERN CRISIS 1945-54
(Select list)

BALL, W. MACMAHON, *Nationalism and Communism in East Asia*. Melbourne University Press, 1952.

BALLANTINE, JOSEPH W., *Formosa: A Problem for United States Foreign Policy*. Washington, The Brookings Institute, 1952.

BARNETT, A. DOAK, *Communist China and Asia: Challenge to American Policy*. New York, Harper, 1960.

BELOFF, MAX, *Soviet Policy in the Far East 1944-1951*. Oxford University Press, 1953.

CLEWS, John C., *The Communists' New Weapon—Germ Warfare*. Lincolns Praeger, 1953.

DULLES, JOHN FOSTER, *Peace with Security: The Texts of Four Major Statements Defining Current American Foreign Policy* (No. 3, Far Eastern Problems, statement of 29 March 1954). United States Information Service, 1954.

EISENHOWER, DWIGHT D., *Mandate for Change 1953–1956*. Heinemann, 1963.

FEIS, HERBERT, *The China Tangle*. Princeton University Press, 1953.

FIFIELD, RUSSELL H. *The Diplomacy of South-East Asia 1945-1958*. New York, Harper, 1958.

GOOLD-ADAMS, RICHARD, *The Time of Power: A Reappraisal of John Foster Dulles*. Weidenfeld and Nicolson, 1962.

GREENE, FELIX, *A Curtain of Ignorance*. Cape, 1965.

HIGGINS, TRUMBULL, *Korea and the Fall of MacArthur*. Oxford University Press, 1960.

LANCASTER, DONALD, *The Emancipation of French Indochina* (chaps. 16 and 17). Oxford University Press, 1961.

LATOURETTE, KENNETH, *The American Record in the Far East, 1945–1951*. New York, Macmillan, 1952.

LEVI, WERNER, *Modern China's Foreign Policy*. University of Minnesota Press, 1953.

MACARTHUR, DOUGLAS, *Reminiscences*. Heinemann, 1964.

PANNIKAR, K. M., *In Two Chinas: Memoirs of a Diplomat*. Allen and Unwin, 1955.

REES, DAVID, *Korea: The Limited War*. Macmillan, 1964.

SPANIER, JOHN W., *The Truman-MacArthur Controversy and the Korean War*. Cambridge, Mass., Belknap Press, 1959.

STONE, ISIDORE F., *The Hidden History of the Korean War*. New York, Monthly Review Press, 1952.

TRUMAN, HARRY S., *Years of Trial and Hope, 1946–1953*. Hodder and Stoughton, 1955.

TSOU, TANG, *America's Failure in China, 1941–50*. University of Chicago Press, 1963.

UNITED STATES, Department of State, *United States Relations with China* (the White Paper). Washington, Government Printing Office, 1949.

VINACKE, Harold M., *The United States and the Far East, 1945–1951*. Stanford University Press, 1952.

WESTERFIELD, H. BRADFORD, *Foreign Policy and Party Politics: Pearl Harbor to Korea* (chaps. 12 and 16). Yale University Press, 1955.

WHITING, ALLEN C., *China Crosses the Yalu*. New York, Macmillan, 1960.

WINT, GUY, *What Happened in Korea? A Study of Collective Security*. Batchworth Press, 1954.

Index

Abyssinia, 26, 32n.

Acheson, Dean, China under 'foreign yoke', 33; not intransigent, 34; policy on Formosa, 69 and n., 82; 'hopping mad', 83; on cease-fire, 117; and Yalu raid, 129; British confidence in, 129, 138

Acland, Sir Richard, challenges Churchill over Greece, 5n.

Addison, Viscount, 51; on people of China, 61

Africa, 19

'Agrarian democrat' theory, 5–8, 11 and n., 15, 145–6

Ailwyn, Lord, 80

Alanbrooke, F.-M. Viscount, on MacArthur, 110n.

Alexander, F.-M. Earl, not told of Yalu raid, 127

Alsace-Lorraine, 80

American opinion, see United States: American opinion

Amery, Julian, West at war with Communism, 71–2; a 'Suez rebel', 72n.; war not provoked, 73–4

Amethyst, H.M.S., 27

ANZUS Pact, 139

Appeasement, 62–3, 86–7, 90, 107, 115, 147, 151

Archibald, Lady, 157

Asia, emancipation of, 8, 145; Mao preaches liberation of, 9; emergent, 13, 28, 45, 85; failure of democracy in, 19; nationalism of, 21, 35, 45, 96, 119, 136–7, 148; European retreat from, 31; touchiness of, 37; opinion of, 37, 39, 42, 47, 70, 105, 109, 142; militarily negligible, 39; and Chinese seat, 49; MacArthur on, 110–11; need of support from, 137; relations with West, 142

Asquith, H. H., government of, 53

Athens, suppression of rising in, 5; ancient, 91

Atomic bomb, 21; Soviet, 22, 56, 85; Asian belief concerning, 38; 'might have saved Chiang', 72; possible employment in Korea, 104–5, 113n., in
N

Indo-China, 136. See also Hydrogen bomb.

Attlee, Clement, 139n, 156; admits peril of war, 72n.; visit to Truman, 75, 105–6, 122; on Formosa, 75, 76n.; on Korean outbreak, 87–8; motion on Korea, 89; censures Churchill, 125–6; policy of revealed, 126; demands Yalu raid debate, 127; on truce talks, 131; on Ho Chi Minh, 134; receives 800 postcards, 159

Australia, 36, 39, 140n.

Austria, 43

Balkans, 10

Beaverbrook press, 86n. See also *Daily Express, Evening Standard*

Berlin Conference, 134

Bevan, Aneurin, challenges Churchill over Greece, 5n.; resignation from cabinet, 64, 108, 124, from shadow cabinet, 139 and n.; on Communism, 124; on American policy, 124–5, 131; stresses economic challenge, 124, 149; against SEATO, 139; ideological affinity with revolutionary Asia, 146; at Peace with China meeting, 160

Bevanites, 89, 123, 128 and n.

Bevin, Ernest, 5n., 156; believes Labour could work with Moscow, 4; on recognition, 25, 36–7; his foreign policy, 30, 148; 'stabbed in back', 30n.; talks with Acheson, 34; and Chinese seat, 46–7, 55, 61; on Soviet boycott of U.N., 46; his hope for U.N., 53; on General Assembly, 55; conciliatory towards China, 58; refusal to identify Chinese people with Communism, 61, 148; proposes Korean peace terms, 97; influence and death, 124

Bing, Geoffrey, 159

Birmingham, Bishop of (Barnes), on napalm bomb, 130n.

Boer War, 31n.

Bow, 158